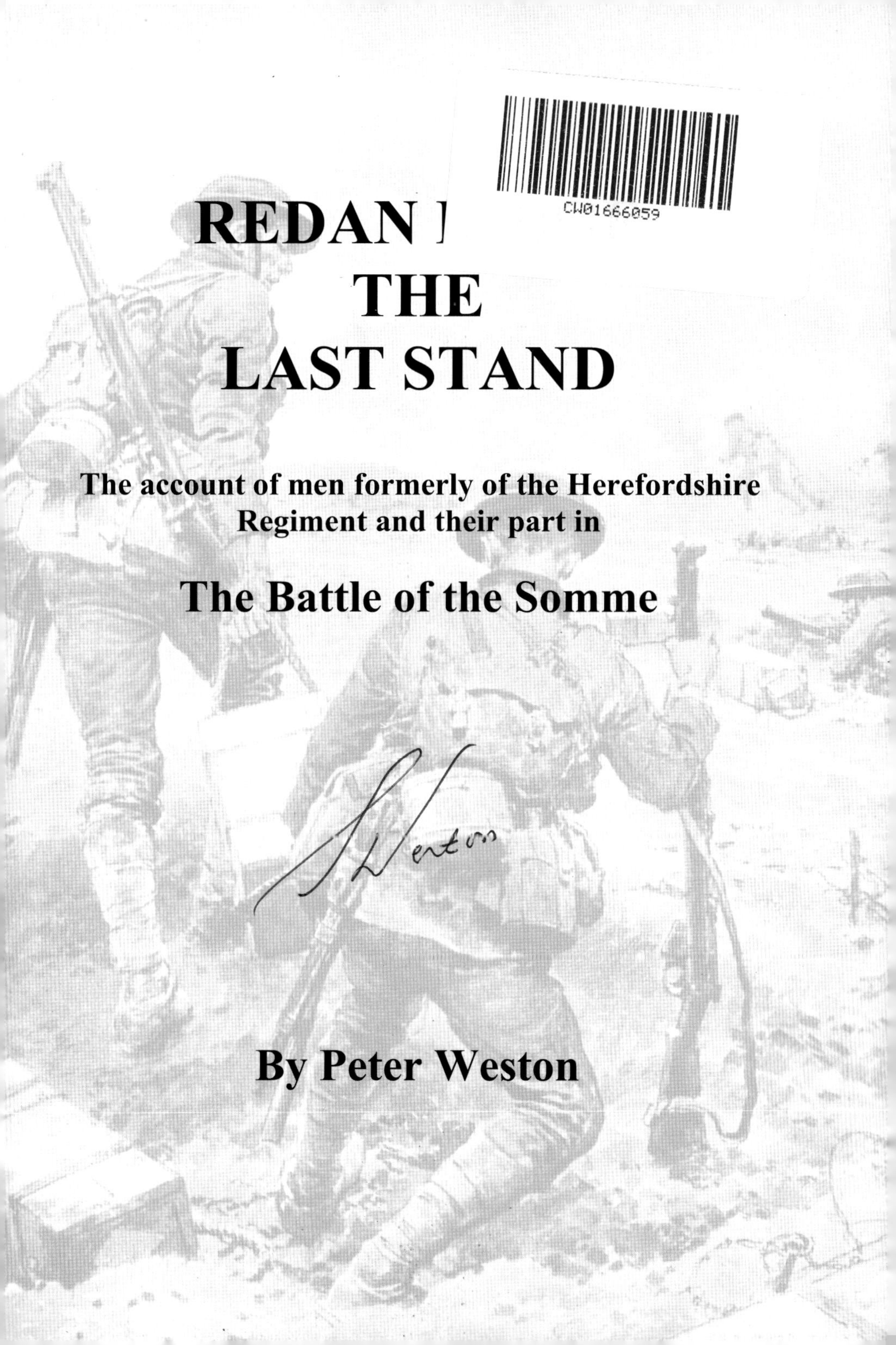

REDAN
THE LAST STAND

The account of men formerly of the Herefordshire Regiment and their part in

The Battle of the Somme

By Peter Weston

First Published in 2005 by Peter Weston
Second revised edition Published in 2012
Leominster
Herefordshire
HR68SQ

Printed by Orphans Press Ltd
Enterprise Park
Leominster
Herefordshire
HR6 0LD

ISBN 978-0-9552477-1-2

This book is dedicated to the memory of the men from Herefordshire who served with the 11th Battalion the Border Regiment

'The Lonsdales'

'Say not that the brave die'

Contents

The Earl's men	7-16
Return to the Somme	17-18
Map showing line of attack	19
The Battle for Frankfort Trench	20-23
Isolated	24-36
Officers Statements	37-52
The Men of Hereford	53-82
The Silent Cities	83-88
Visiting the battlefields today	89-112
Roll of Honour	113-116
Acknowledgments	117
Bibliography	118
Abbreviations	119
The Earl and Countess of Lonsdale 1928	120
Notes	121-124

Introduction

With the publication of the first edition of this book in 2005, I believed the epic tale of the Last Stand on Redan Ridge had been told. However in the years since its publication I have come to realise that it was perhaps not the end but merely just the beginning, and that a story never truly ends.
Seven years have now passed since I first published my book and countless people have kindly contacted me with their family stories and accounts, and further research through the many sources of records on-line have provided more and more information making this second revised edition possible.
I have tried my best to keep the book in its original format using the age old maxim of if it's not broken don't try to fix it. The statements and accounts made by the people who were there at the time have been reproduced in their own words. With ninety six years having passed since this action occurred I would like to think that this time I have finally got to the bottom of the story but I am sure that there is still more to come.
Finally, I would like to express my sincere thanks to all those who have contributed information and accounts and who have helped to make this second edition possible.

Pete Weston

The Fifth Earl of Lonsdale

The Earl's men

High on an open wind swept ridge north of Beaucourt and east of Beaumont-Hamel stand a group of small Somme battlefield cemeteries. In November 1916 thirty five year old Benjamin Bounds from Kington in Herefordshire was reported as missing in action. Several months would pass before his family received official notification of his death. He now lies at peace in Wagon Road Cemetery[1] along with 49 of his comrades from the 11th Battalion the Border Regiment who died in the war to end all wars.

Of all the battles fought during the Great War perhaps the most infamous would be the Battle of the Somme. This battle which commenced on the 1st July 1916 would formally come to a close after four bitter months of fighting on the18th Nov 1916.

Much has been written about the first day of the battle, however little has been put on paper concerning the last day and the events that took place from the 18th to 25th November 1916 on Redan Ridge.

At the start of the war many believed that hostilities would be over by Christmas 1914 but the newly appointed Secretary of State for war, Field Marshal Lord Kitchener, predicted that the war could last for up to three years. Britain's small professional peacetime army would need to be bolstered by new recruits. One idea that was suggested as a way of encouraging men to join the colours was to promise that friends who joined up together could train and serve together. Soon hundreds of men, encouraged by local communities, clubs and societies, rushed to answer their country's call for volunteers. Numerous new battalions (Bns) were formed, some commonly referred to as Pal's Battalions taking their names from the cities, clubs and societies which the men represented such as Glasgow Boys Brigade, Hull Commercials, Grimsby Chums. What had not

[1] The spelling of Wagon Road is that used in Official War diaries and reports of the day

been visualised was that whole communities would be shocked to learn that just as these young men had joined up and trained together so would many become casualties together on the killing fields of the Somme and Passchendaele. In many cases whole battalions were all but wiped out. This slaughter would change Britain forever having devastating consequences on the generation who went to fight in the Great War. Few families would not loose a son or other family member or in some way be unaffected by the terrible carnage.

The fifth Earl of Lonsdale[2] was keen that a Pals battalion be formed from the local men of Cumberland and Westmoreland. Within days hundreds of men from all manner of trades and professions such as shepherds, miners and farm workers rushed to sign up. To command and train the newly formed battalion the Earl selected 52 year old Colonel Percy Matchell,[3] a retired army officer of many years experience.

Taking an enthusiastic interest in the battalion not only did the Earl design a smart grey uniform for the men he even financed it from his own pocket. Unfortunately, his chosen colour of grey proved to be a poor selection as this was also the colour used by the enemy (this was later changed to the standard British khaki uniform).

Officially raised on the 17th September 1914, the battalion was designated the 11th Bn the Border Regiment, the Lonsdales. Training commenced at Carlisle racecourse where the men were taught basic instruction and drill. As the battalion grew from strength to strength, bigger and better training locations were sought and the men found themselves moving around the country receiving tuition in the art of musketry and warfare. Finally, in August 1915, the battalion was declared

---

[2] Often referred to as the Yellow Earl it is reputed that the Automobile Association adopted his distinctive yellow heraldic colours as a background colour.
He is though perhaps better known for his patronage to the sport of boxing and the Lonsdale Belt championship.

[3] Colonel Matchell had served for a number of years with the Essex Regiment and in Egypt.

ready for overseas service and on the 23rd November set sail for France aboard the troopship 'Princess Victoria'. For most of the recruits this would be the adventure of a lifetime many never having travelled further than local fairs and markets, shortly they would find themselves in a foreign land.

Lord Lonsdale centre (carrying cane) with Colonel Matchell (far right) inspecting the men.

The war on the Western Front had by this time become deadlocked with hundreds of miles of opposing trenches stretching from the Belgian coast to the borders of Switzerland. The German forces commenced the construction of deep underground defences whilst the British and French considered that their defensive positions were only temporary. The German strategy of defence as opposed the allied view of offence would later prove to have dramatic consequences for both Britain and France.

On the 21st February 1916, German troops attacked the French fortified city of Verdun. The German plan, codenamed 'Gericht'-'a place of execution', was based on the belief that

France would defend Verdun to the last man. Germany would quite simply bleed the French army to death. The battle raged on for ten bitter months. When the conflict finally ended in December the frontline had barely moved, but France had sustained 540,000 casualties. The German army had also incurred massive casualties, suffering losses of over 430,000.

The battle for Verdun was crippling the French army and to try to relief the pressure France demanded action from her British allies. Plans had already been prepared several months earlier for a new offensive on the Somme region of the frontline. Britain had many thousands of newly trained troops on the Western-Front. If an attack was made by a joint British and French force on the Somme then several French divisions could be released to assist at Verdun.

On the 1st July 1916, the 11th Borderers would, along with many other battalions, take part on the opening day of the battle. This day would prove to be the blackest in British military history.

For six days prior to the start of the battle 1,500 British guns constantly pounded the German lines, firing over 150,000 shells in every twenty-four hour period. Eventually the breeches of some of the guns became so hot that they had to use axes to break them open. On many guns the persistent recoil caused the buffer springs to snap under the tremendous strain. Even this relentless bombardment had failed to break the German defences; deep in underground bunkers the enemy awaited the infantry attack.

Believing the Germans had all but been annihilated by the ferocious artillery barrage, thousands of ‘Tommies’ left the relative safety of their trenches and headed across no man’s land towards the enemy frontline. By the end of this day 60,000 would become casualties. The next day a further 40,000 would add to the now bursting field hospitals and casualty clearing stations.

At 7.30hrs precisely on the 1st July the artillery barrage ceased and for a few seconds there was an eerie silence, this was soon followed by whistle blasts from officers who encouraged the men to leave their trenches and advance towards the enemy.

For some this whistle blast would be the last earthly sound they would ever hear. The 11th Borderers were due to take part in the second wave of the attack which was scheduled to start thirty minutes later at 8.00am. Colonel Matchell, the commanding officer of the Lonsdales, issued the order for the men to commence their advance towards the starting point on the edge of Authuille Wood. The Germans had by now climbed up from their deep dugouts and had set up their Maxim guns. Emotions were tense and as the men set off several shook hands and wished each other well, some even cheered. But at the very moment that they exited from the wood to commence their advance they came under heavy sustained machine gun fire from two strong points forming part of the German defences know as the *Nordwerk* and the *Granatloch*.

'Will any of us ever forget the journey that morning? just to the right front of Rock Street gun pit the Royal Engineers had cut a gap in the hedge on the edge of the wood, and through this gap marched our infanteers the 11th Borderers and the 1st Dorset's to be mown down by Jerry's machine guns as fast as they marched through'. 'The wood was being heavily shelled, and clambering on to the Artillery Bridge we found a slaughter-house'. [4]

The Borderers lay strewn all around and through the opening, from which they had rushed, formed a brown patch created by the heaped khaki clad bodies of the dead and wounded British Tommies. Perhaps Colonel Matchell had predicted the destiny

---

[4] Account made by an unknown witness serving with the RA.
Artillery and Trench Mortar Memories, 32nd Division. R.Whinyates 1932.

of the Lonsdales on that fateful morning as the day preceding the attack he had been heard to say:

The track and opening on the edge of the wood from where the Lonsdales exited on the 1st July 1916 (Author's collection 2005).

'If things go badly, I'll come up and see it through.' 'Everyone was tense as no messages were received from the companies. The Colonel was fidgeting and watching the progress of his men and eventually decided to go and lead them himself but as soon as he left the trench he was shot through the head and killed. Then the Adjutant was severely wounded as he leant over the Colonels body. The second in command had already been wounded. The C.O.'s batman, his bugler and two runners were all killed but I was only knocked over by a shell and stunned'.[5]

---

[5] Account by L/Cpl.F.Allan. Field clerk 11th Borderers regarding 1st July attack. The first day on the Somme. Martin Middlebrook. Penguin Books 1971.

Grave of Colonel P W. Matchell
In Warloy-Baillon cemetery

Colonel Percy Wilfred Matchell Commanding Officer 11th Battalion Border Regiment Killed in action 1st July 1916. (Author's collection.)

Throughout the day stretcher bearers constantly risked their lives clambering from the trenches into no man's land searching for injured men. Some of the wounded had managed to find refuge in shell holes and lay waiting in the baking sun for darkness and the opportunity to try to crawl back to the British front-line. Those who could not wait dashed for safety only to face the relentless swathes of machine gun fire and the deadly aim of the tiresome snipers.

Of the 823 Borderers who set off that morning only 305 remained at roll call at the days end. 10 officers were dead a further 15 were wounded.

Now commanded by Lieutenant Welsh the remaining members of the battalion were withdrawn back to Authuille Dump.

Despite the terrible massacre which they had all faced the battle weary troops were promptly put to work carrying up grenades and stores to the front.

The battalion continued to carryout fatigue duties for the next few days. During the 8th July they were marched to Senlis, and Captain Palmer of the 2nd Kings Own Yorkshire Light Infantry took over provisional command as the C.O. from Lt Welsh.

The Lonsdales had by now been reorganised in to two companies and the battalion strength was recorded as 11 officers and 480 other ranks. On the 9th July ninety men were ordered to carry out a trench raid, bearing in mind that just days previously the Lonsdales had lost almost all of their officers and upwards of nearly five hundred other ranks. It is perhaps not so surprising that thirty reported sick, saying they were suffering from shell shock. The C.O. arranged a sick parade at 11.pm, following examination of the men the medical officer Lieutenant Kirkwood wrote out the following certificate.[6]

'In view of the bombing raid to be carried out by the 11th Border Regiment, I must herby testify to their unfitness for such an operation as few, if any are not suffering from some degree of shell shock'. [7]

Despite the medical advice given by Lt Kirkwood the trench raid was still ordered to take place. The party was led towards the jumping-off point by Second Lieutenant Ross who later reported that there was ***'a great lack of offensive spirit in the party'.***[8] It was suggested that the men had moved so slowly and reluctantly towards the jumping-off point that it had been

---

[6] The Realities of war Philip Gibbs (London Heinemann 1920)

[7] Court of enquiry into the failure of a party of the 11th Border Regiment to carry out an attack on 10th July 1916. Wellcome History of Medicine, RAMC 446/18.

[8] Court of enquiry into failure of a party of 11th Border Regiment to carry out an attack on 10th July 1916.

impossible to keep to the original timetable, and as a result S/Lt Ross had to cancel the raid and was forced to return.

Following S/Lt Ross's report four sergeants from the party were arrested and a Court of enquiry was convened. At the enquiry Lt Kirkwood the M.O. explained that he believed that the men were totally demoralized following the 1st July and that they had not had sufficient time to recover their equilibrium. His point of view was not accepted by either the brigade of divisional commanders who said that the M.O. was to blame for the debacle and that he should be relived of his duties. General Hubert Gough, commanding the Reserve Army wrote;

'It is inconceivable how men, who have pledged themselves to fight and uphold the honour of their country, could degrade themselves in such a manner, and show an utter want of manly spirit and courage which, at least is expected of every soldier and Britisher. The conduct on the part of Lt Kirkwood RAMC shows him to be totally unfitted to hold a commission in the army, or to exercise any military responsibility. Immediate steps must be taken to remove Lt Kirkwood from the service'. [9]

The Army Director of Medical services asked General Gough to reconsider, but he was adamant that Lt Kirkwood should go. In the case file is a note written by the Surgeon General Sir Arthur Sloggett, it states

'The whole case is deplorable. The M.O. appears to have been made a scapegoat'.

The battalion diary records that on the12th July Lt Kirkwood was removed as the M.O. and replaced by Lt Webster. Just five days later General Rycroft the Divisional Commander addressed the Brigade and congratulated them on their achievements.

---

[9] Court of Enquiry into failure of a party of 11th Border Regiment to carry out an attack on 10th July 1916.

By the end of July the Lonsdales had left the Somme. Replacements, training and re-supply of vital equipment were now urgently needed before the battalion could return to full operational fighting strength. Over the next few months the men carried out duties as working parties carrying supplies, digging trenches and periods of frontline trench duties. Training and re-supply continued as well as drafts of new men to make good the losses of the 1st July.

In late September of 1916 somewhere in the region of 200 to 300 men from the 3rd Battalion the Herefordshire Regiment, which had been formed as a reserve battalion were transferred to the Lonsdales for service overseas in France. There was no time to waste these valuable reserves would shortly be needed to carry on the struggle, and would quickly have to adapt to the harsh realities of trench warfare. Within weeks the men were formed into effective front line fighting soldiers, undertaking periods of instruction and spells of duty at the front.

A group of men of the Herefordshire Regiment undergoing training at Oswestry (Author's collection)

Return to the Somme

The Battle of the Somme had raged on since the 1st July and now, as winter quickly approached and weather conditions deteriorated, the military planners concluded that if there was to be any hope of smashing the German defences and securing a victory on the Somme one last major push was required. By now the fertile fields of the Somme had been turned into a sea of mud and shell holes, the landscape littered with debris, churned up by the many thousands of shells fired by both attacker and defender alike.

Towards the end of October the Lonsdales returned to the Somme. During the early part of November they took part in several Brigade field days where they practiced open country movement, and undertook a number of route marches.

Early in November the village of Beaumont-Hamel had finally been captured but the enemy still dominated the area from a formidable vantage point on the high ground called Redan Ridge. If the enemy frontline could be breached the battle could still yet be won. This would be the final operation in the Somme campaign and the job of completing this task was given to the 32nd Division. Before them lay the daunting German frontline defences of Munich and Frankfort Trenches on Redan Ridge[10]. As part of the 97th Infantry Brigade, the 11th Borderers, along with the 16th and 17th Highland Light Infantry and the 2nd Kings Own Yorkshire Light Infantry, were ordered to make preparations to take part in the attack which was scheduled to commence at 6.10 am on the morning of the 18th of November.

---

[10] The spelling of Frankfort is sometimes changed to Frankfurt; in fact the battle field cemetery on Redan Ridge is spelt Frankfurt.

The men from Herefordshire along with their colleagues from Cumberland and Westmorland were soon to experience the full horrors of war. On the 15th the Lonsdales were ordered to dump their packs and parade in battle order, at 2.00pm they commenced their march to Englebelmer arriving at 5.00pm.

The next day the 16th was spent fitting out with bombs and making final preparations. At 11.00pm on the night of the 17th, in full fighting order, the Lonsdales commenced the long march through the village of Mailly-Maillet and on to an area behind the British front-line known as 'White City'. From this point led by the C.O. they passed over open country and made their way towards the trenches opposite Wagon Road. Once in position the battalion relieved members of the East Lancashire and North Lancashire Regiments. The relief was at long last completed by 1.00am but not without incident, the German artillery had constantly shelled the area causing several casualties. Later that day the C.O. visited Brigade HQ and received his final orders, upon his return he held a meeting with all the company commanders briefing them of what course of action the battalion would undertake in the forthcoming attack. At midnight the C.O. and the Adjutant laid a white tape in the direction of Wagon Road for the men to follow. Shortly after 5.00am the Lonsdales were in position and ready. But for many others of the 97th Brigade it was a very different story. Having set off at 9.45 pm on the night of the 17th to make their way to the starting off point, they would not arrive until minutes before the attack commenced.

Throughout the night the weather turned for the worse and snow started to fall, half frozen and exhausted units soon became disorientated. Despite the best efforts of guides whose job was to try to ensure the men arrived safely at the starting off point many became lost. Finally after six long hours the last stragglers arrived at the assembly point.

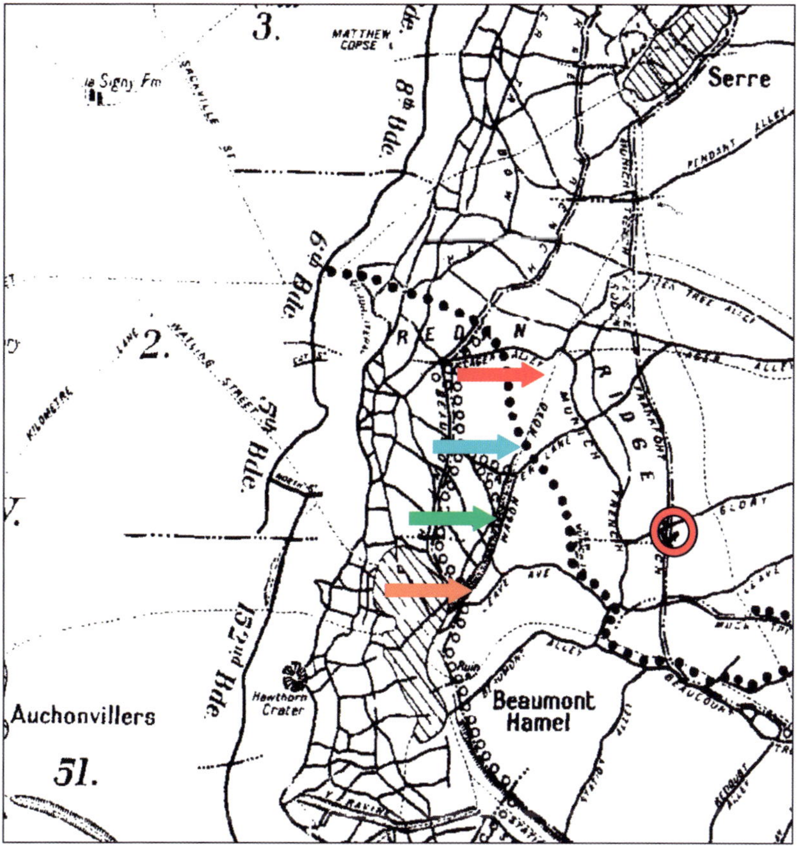

MAP SHOWING LINE OF ATTACK 97th BRIGADE
18th NOVEMBER 1916

2nd K O Y L I

11th BORDER REG

16th H L I

17th H L I

N

97th Brigade line of attack = 1,125 yds front

STRONG POINT ◯ IN FRANKFORT TRENCH 18th-25th

The Battle for Frankfort Trench

View looking up Wagon Road (Author's collection 2005)

Everything was now in place. At 6.10am the British Artillery barrage started, signalling the opening of the battle to capture Redan Ridge. Each man had been issued with 220 rounds of ammunition; in addition some also had to carry extra equipment such as bombs and stores. The average man carried in excess of 56 lbs and in some cases this represented nearly a third of the typical soldier's body weight.

Encouraged by their officers the Lonsdales and the other accompanying battalions scrambled out of their positions and started to move off towards the enemy lines.

The churned up mud and snow hampered the advance and a freezing blizzard of sleet added to the bitterly cold conditions.

Artist's impression of troops storming an enemy trench

The 17th Bn of the HLI who were on the extreme right flank of the 97th Brigade's attack had earlier crawled out to a location in front of New Munich Trench. Unfortunately, the British barrage fell short killing and wounding many of the men of the 17th HLI. Comparatively untouched the Germans holding Munich Trench opened up with both machine gun and rifle fire forcing many of the 17th HLI to fall back. The 16th HLI faired better, the barrage being far more effective on their front, allowing many of the men to cross right over Munich Trench their first objective, and carry on to Frankfort Trench. The Lonsdales also suffered from the British barrage falling short. The C.O. of the battalion later wrote.

'To say the British barrage was ineffective is too mild altogether'.

Despite the setbacks a number of Lonsdales also succeeded in crossing over Munich Trench and joining the men of the 16th HLI fighting to hold a section of Frankfort Trench.

On the extreme left of the attack the 2nd KOYLI were held back by heavy machine gun fire, but in the end a number did manage to break through. What now followed was fierce hand to hand fighting by all the men involved in the bitter struggle to capture and consolidate any gains.

Following the initial successes made by the 97th Brigade the enemy now mounted a determined counter attack, unable to sustain their positions the remaining British troops still fighting out in the open were forced to retreat back to Wagon Road abandoning Munich Trench as they went. However neither side realised that just 2-3 hundred yards to the rear of Munich Trench were a party of men from the 16th HLI and 11th Borderers cut off in a captured section of Frankfort Trench.

'No Man's Land' between us and Fritz was nothing but shell holes and we went from one to another like playing hide and seek. I played it pretty well until I got close to the Bosch and then a piece of shrapnel caught me in the thigh and I lost interest in the game for a bit. I lay in a shell hole all day 'under fire' waiting for dark. As soon as it was dark enough I left my way being enlivened by a few parting shots from a sniper who had taken a kindly interest in me all day, and wasted a lot of good ammunition in his attempts to show it. I got through it all right although I was under shell fire for a time after Mr Sniper had ceased from troubling me. While waiting for dark I had plenty of chance to watch our artillery at work and I was almost sorry for Fritz. It seemed almost impossible that anything could live under that rain of shell. They had got the range almost to an inch'. [11]

---

[11] Extract from a letter sent by Private C Haynes 11th Borderers formally 3rd Bn Herefordshire Regiment from Stretford Bridge Dilwyn to his parents. Reproduced in the Leominster News in October 1916.

In the closing hours of the 18th the last stragglers and walking wounded tried as best they could to make their way back to Wagon Road.

Throughout the day the battalion stretcher-bearers had bravely carried the wounded in broad daylight whilst constantly been sniped at by the enemy. In the case of the 16th HLI over half had themselves become casualties.

Fearing for the safety of his men the Bn doctor had to appeal to the C.O. to intervene to prevent their complete annihilation. By night the battlefield became even more perilous as the bearers tried to negotiate their way around the debris that littered the battlefield. Many of the wounded still lay out in the open. Some had managed to take refuge in one of the many shell craters. Guided by the pitiful cries for help the bearers frantically searched around to locate the injured. But as dawn broke there was now little hope of any further rescue. The lucky ones might be found by enemy patrols and taken in.

Artist's impression of the tireless work of the stretcher-bearers

The final battle of the 1916 Somme campaign was now all but over, however for some cut off in enemy held territory the battle was to continue for several more days.

ISOLATED

What was left of the battle weary 97th Infantry Brigade were withdrawn back to Wagon Road and regrouped in case the enemy counter-attacked. In the meantime the group of defenders still holding out in Frankfort Trench set about consolidating that position.

Estimates as to the exact number who occupied Frankfort Trench vary, however one official report puts the figure at seven officers and one hundred and twenty three other ranks[12]. Comprising of the following, three officers and sixty other ranks from both the 16th Bn HLI and 11th Bn Borders, and one officer and three other ranks from the 2nd Bn KOYLI.

Frankfort Trench was in a very poor state of repair having been virtually flattened by the tremendous British artillery bombardment. Within the trench were two dugouts it was decided to place the wounded which at this time approximately fifty into the smaller of the two dugouts, whilst the remainder of effective men occupied the other.

The defenders were surrounded on all sides but as yet the Germans were totally unaware of their presence. Rapid action was now needed; once the enemy was to become aware of their existence the defenders would surely find themselves in a perilous situation. Taking stock of available stores revealed that four Lewis guns and a limited amount of ammunition were at hand. In order to supplement supplies men handed in their rifle ammunition to the Lewis gunners and in turn rearmed themselves from a ready supply of German Mauser rifles and cartridges found within the trench. Water was collected from shell holes and boiled on makeshift lamps made from tins filled with gun oil using strips of flannelette as a wick.

---

[12] Report by Major R. Rowan. On the situation of a party of the 97th Inf. Bde. In Frankfort Trench, 21 November 1916; 32nd Division, "Narrative of Operations"; "Report on Operations carried out by the 32nd Division from Nov.19th to 24th", all PRO WO 95/2368.

A good number of the wounded were in a desperate state, some with fractured bones exposed to the elements. Others had hideous lacerations. Field dressings were the only available bandages, and in most cases these proved to be hopelessly inadequate with the more serious wounds. No one amongst the group had anything other than a limited working knowledge of first aid. A corporal was placed in charge of the casualties, but all that could be done in most cases was to attempt to make the injured as comfortable as possible and hope for the best.

19th November 1916 Day Two

By the morning of day two essential repairs had been undertaken in an effort to prevent the trench from collapsing. The four Lewis guns were positioned at vital strategic points, and the men who were considered fighting fit were organised into teams. One-hour sentry duty followed by two hours relief ensured that a constant watch was kept on the enemy positions. In the event that the defenders were discovered a swift response could follow.

Despite slightly improved conditions within the trench the state of the wounded was becoming worse by the hour. Many of the injured were in a frightful state requiring urgent medical attention. Wounds were quickly becoming infected, and no pain killing drugs or clean bandages available.

The majority of the men had by now drank their water rations and had eaten what food they had. As night fell volunteers crept out into no-man's land gathering what ever they could find from the dead. As yet the enemy was still unaware that just yards away the small garrison were holding out waiting for relief. Surely the defenders thought a rescue party would be sent to bring them to safety, but perhaps not even the British were aware of their existence. All that could be done was to wait and hope.

20th November 1916 Day Three

Whilst the defenders anxiously waited, the enemy were growing suspicious. Perhaps they were alerted by noise or movement and decided to send a raiding party to investigate. What was to follow was a desperate battle.

Once discovered, the Germans commenced bombing the trench, bravely the defenders returned with both rifle and machine gun fire. Fearing the worst men armed themselves with entrenching tools ready for close-quarter hand-to-hand fighting. Greatly out numbered the defenders put up such a bitter struggle that the enemy having lost many men eventually retreated back to the safety of the German lines. The initial euphoria of having beaten off a determined assault was tempered when the defenders realised that they too had sustained several more casualties, further depleting the ability to defend the trench.

The wounded now out-numbered the able and, in order to maximise what few effective fighting men were left, it was decided to abandon the smaller of the two dugouts containing the injured and consolidate the force into the larger dugout.

During the past three days, two individuals of the 16th Bn HLI had distinguished themselves, demonstrating exceptional skills of leadership and had constantly throughout been a source of encouragement to all the men. Both Sergeant George Lee, who before the war had been employed by Glasgow Corporation as a roads foreman, and Lance-Corporal John Veitch who had played a major role in successfully deploying the Lewis guns would later be recommended for the award of the Victoria Cross.[13] Sadly both would perish, but were later awarded posthumous Mention in Despatches.

---

[13] Both the bodies of Sgt G. Lee and L/Cpl J. Veitch were lost, or never identified. Having no know grave they are both commemorated on the Thiepval Memorial to the Missing on the Somme.

The Breakout

Artist's impression of Lewis gunners defending a position

During the night of the 20th, Company Sergeant Major (CSM) Johnstone and Private Dixon of the 11th Borderers crept out of the trench and managed to break through to the British line. Upon his safe return on the morning of the 21st CSM Johnstone was conveyed to Brigade HQ at White City where he was able to inform the authorities of the plight of the defenders holding out in Frankfort Trench.[14] In his report he stated that some of the Border and HLI officers and men were still holding a portion of Frankfort Trench. Based upon this information it was decided to put together a rescue party, made up equally of one officer and thirty other ranks from each of the two battalions involved (Border-HLI).

---

[14] 11th Border Regiment: War Diary, November 21st 1916. PRO WO 95/2403
The war diary makes mentions of Captain Welch. Border Regiment cut off in Frankfort-Trench, in other publications his name is spelt Welsh.

21st November 1916 Day Four

As the siege continued hopes began to rise when a British observation aircraft was spotted flying low over the beleaguered garrison. Believing that perhaps CSM Johnston and Pte Dixon had been successful in their escape, the defenders considered that the aircraft was indeed trying to pin-point their exact location. Desperate to make contact, a signaller daringly crawled out into no mans land and lay on his back in a hollow. Using pieces of a torn shirt he frantically tried to attract the pilot's attention. Suddenly the aircraft turned and headed back towards the British line, hearts sank and expectations faded as the men started to suspect that the pilot had not seen them. After a short period the aircraft returned accompanied by several other aircraft, using torches the pilots began signalling to the men. Four days of struggle had reduced the defenders to a pitiful condition, suffering from lack of food and water as well as deprived of sleep most were now physically exhausted. Many of the wounded were beyond help and lay silent waiting to die, with every hour the situation grew more and more desperate as wounds became infected and turned gangrenous. But encouraged by the fact that the British now certainly knew of their position the men grew optimistic that relief was on the way.

British B.E.2cs used by 15 Squadron RFC

The aircraft that had discovered the defenders belonged to 15 Squadron Royal Flying Corps.
The squadron had been formed on the 1st March 1915 at Farnborough Airfield and had been equipped with Royal Aircraft Company B.E.2cs recognisance aircraft, supplemented with a few Bristol Scout planes.
On 22nd December 1915 the Squadron moved to France and began operating in a reconnaissance role in support of the IV Army. Throughout the Somme campaign 15 Sqd suffered heavy losses from both German fighter aircraft and ground fire.

On the morning of the 21st the 32nd Division War Diary records that at 12.15pm the Squadron Commander of 15 Sqd was telephoned and asked to try to communicate with the marooned party. The following day 22nd the diary records that an officer of 15 Sqd was ordered to fly over the marooned party and signal "C.I. Night'' on his return he telephoned Division and reported seeing the men, who waved flags to him, but he was uncertain if they had acknowledged his signal.
He was subsequently ordered to again fly over the area and on his return give a report on the German trenches in the neighbourhood.[15]
At 9.30 pm that evening, guided by CSM Johnstone, the relief party of two officers and sixty men drawn from both the Borderers and HLI set off from Wagon Road, and headed towards the enemy frontline. Commanded by Captain Hunter 11th Borderers and Lieutenant Crichton 16th HLI, the party made their way up to the German wire in front of Munich Trench. CSM Johnstone proceeded to work his way along the wire South to North. But due to the darkness and the fact that there was a prevailing ground mist, he was unable to find a suitable gap in the wire through which the party could pass.

[15] Extracts taken from Intelligence Summary War Diary /32nd Division 21-22nd Nov 1916. The National Archive Kew.

Fearing that at any moment the party may be discovered by a passing enemy patrol Captain Hunter reluctantly took the decision to withdraw returning back to Wagon Road at 4.30 am on the morning of the 22nd.

22nd November 1916 Day Five

The previous night had brought a heavy barrage causing a great deal of destruction. Doing the best they could the defenders tried their best to make good the damage and remain vigilant. Later in the day, a British aircraft flew over the trench dropping a bag, but as it fell towards the ground the wind tore it open. Horrified the men could only watch as the bag and its contents were blow into the enemy trenchers. The pilot observing what had happened signalled by torch the message "coming tomorrow" but some in the trench read it as "come in tomorrow". Confused and unsure of what action to now take the defenders pondered as to their fate. Should they attempt a breakout or wait in anticipation of a rescue force coming to their assistance. With the passage of time it is not totally clear as to what if any decision was taken, but some reports suggest that a further two men had escaped from the trench. Indicating to the authorities that it was the intention of the defenders to try to break out that night. It may possibly have been that the British pilot's intention was merely to attempt to confirm or even suggest what course of action the defenders may take.

Both the Official War Diaries of the 11th Borderers and the 16th HLI, state that following the failure of the first rescue attempt. A second rescue mission was planned, this time each Bn would supply one officer and fifty other ranks. Believing that at some point in the night the defenders intended breaking out, the rescue party was ordered to position themselves in trenches close to Wagon Road some two hundred yards from the enemy line. The group was instructed to hold itself in readiness and to give assistance to the defenders in the event that they attempted to break through. By 8.30 pm the party was in position and lay in wait until 06.00am the following morning.

As dawn broke it was clear that the second rescue had not been successful. The 97th Brigade was finally relieved on the afternoon of the 23rd by the 96th Brigade. As the defenders' comrades were marched back to their billets well behind the British line any hope of rescue would now fall onto the men of the 96th Brigade.

23rd November 1916 Day Six

Artist's impression of a trench under attack by the enemy

The Germans now began to grow impatient of this defiant group holding out in their trench system, and on the afternoon of the sixth day launched a furious attack from the front and both flanks.

Exhausted and weary, the defenders alerted by the enemy shelling made their way up from their dugout ready to meet the foe. The enemy was fresh and well fed unlike the poor souls preparing to fight to the last. What followed was a truly magnificent effort by the defenders; fierce hand to hand fighting resulted in the enemy being routed. Not only had the men successfully beaten off the determined German attack, but they had also in the process captured eight prisoners.

Whilst the defenders prepared themselves for further enemy attacks, L/Cpl Veitch remained at the ready manning his Lewis gun. But a German sniper had him in his sights; suddenly L/Cpl Veitch fell dead to the floor having been struck in the head by a sniper's bullet. This was a bitter blow to all; throughout he had displayed courage and determination.

The last rescue attempt

As the defenders awaited their fate, yet another rescue plan was been put into operation. This time three companies of the 16th Lancashire Fusiliers and one company of the 2nd Royal Inniskilling Fusiliers from the 96th Brigade, were selected to perform the rescue mission. Zero hour had been set for 3.30pm on the 23rd.

Shortly before noon the British opened up an artillery barrage, in an effort to cut the wire in front of the German line. The attack got off to a good start with the initial wave of troops reaching Munich Trench with little opposition. Regrettably, the remnants of the enemy wire and condition of the ground resulted in the men of the initial wave arriving at different times. From this point on, the attack started to falter, the initial wave eventually entered the trench and commenced to try to gain control from the enemy. Meanwhile the second wave crossed over Munich Trench and carried on towards their final objective.

Unfortunately they became caught up in their own artillery barrage causing them to temporarely halt. Within minutes they came under heavy sustained German machine gun fire, forcing them to retire back to Munich Trench.

A ferocious fight ensued but in the end they were unable to continue the battle. At 4.20 pm the men withdrew, seven officers and two hundred and twenty four men were lost in the final bid to rescue the defenders of Frankfort Trench. Their fate was sealed; the defenders were now effectively abandoned with little hope of rescue.

24th November 1916 Day Seven

As day broke the defenders were alerted to the sight of yet more fresh enemy troops making their way over the communication trenches in preparation for another attack.

Under the cover of a white flag the German commander sent a message carried by an Inniskilling Fusilier captured the previous day in the failed rescue attempt. The message read "surrender and you are assured of good treatment" if they didn't he added menacingly, then German forces would come over in staggering force and they could take what was coming to them. Deserted and with little hope of rescue the bold defenders were all but finished but remained defiant and determined to stand to the last man.

Ignoring the enemy offer the German commander soon responded by shelling the trench, fearing that this was to be the final attack CSM Lee jumped up on to the parapet encouraging the men to fight on. Moments later he was struck by a shell splinter mortally wounding him. It is said that as he lay dying he shouted out "No Surrender". Still the men refused to give in, throughout that night volunteers sneaked out in search of food and water. Upon their return several bottles filled with water collected from a pool in a shell crater were offered up to the

corporal caring for the wounded. On inspection he refused to give it to his patients, by this time some of the men were so desperate with thirst that they drank the water willingly
Those wretched poor devils that did succumb to thirst later contracted typhoid.

25th November 1916 the Final Day

German patience finally ran out on the 25th. From all points of the compass came intensive enemy fire. Shocked and stunned by the strength of the attack the defenders struggled to fight off bombers who constantly delivered their deadly loads, reeking havoc with no care or consideration for the sick and wounded. This was to be a fight to the death. Only after hearing the cries for mercy from the eight German prisoners captured in a previous attack did the enemy stop their ferocious assault.

The last stand was over, of the one hundred and twenty or so who had started off eight days earlier only fifteen unwounded staggered out from the trench dazed and in a state of shock. Barely able to stand, weakened by the effects of lack of food, water and sleep. As they tried their best to remain upright a German officer promptly demanded that they carry out the wounded from within the trench. This was but the start of their ordeal, compelled to march the defenders were taken off deep into enemy held territory where they were interrogated.
Keen to come face to face with his opponents the German Brigadier in command surveyed the men stood before him. In astonishment he said ***'Is this what has held up the Brigade for more than a week?'***

This was undoubtedly a complement to the sheer determination and professionalism of the British Tommies who stood before him. The survivors were taken off into captivity, and the wounded taken to field hospitals. Of the fifteen unwounded two later died as prisoners of the Kaiser.

Reports claim that another was shot for accepting a piece of bread from a French inhabitant.

The whole story of the defiant stand in Frankfort Trench would not be fully told until after the Armistice in 1918, when the prisoners were repatriated and could finally give their personal accounts of there epic actions. In recognition of this remarkable episode Colonel Kyle Commanding Officer 16th. HLI recommended the following awards. One Distinguished Service Order, eleven Distinguished Conduct Medals and twenty-two Military Medals.

General H.P. Gough commander of the Fifth Army wrote to the War Office backing the recommendations.

[16]***'I have received to-day a visit from Colonel Kyle 16th HLI, and he has shown me his recommendations in regard to the attack by his battalion on 18th November 1916. I can confirm all his statements as regards the circumstances of the attack. It was made under immense difficulties of ground and weather. It demanded the greatest grit and courage. I can also confirm the fact of the portion of the battalion which succeeded in capturing the final objective holding out and repelling several attacks during eight days and eventually having to be abandoned after failure of several attempts at relief. I consider that these men deserve great recognition for the magnificent example of soldierly qualities they displayed'.***

The French Government also wishing to acknowledge the achievements of the 16th HLI awarded the Commanding Officer Colonel Kyle, the Cross of the Legion of Honour, which he accepted on behalf of all the men of the battalion.

---

[16] Extract from A Saga of Scotland, History of the 16th Battalion the Highland Light Infantry Thomas Chalmers. Published by John McCallum and Co. page 67. However Chalmers makes no reference to any awards to other battalions who were involved in this action.

General SIR H, de la POER GOUGH, KCB.KCVO.

The commander of the Fifth army which fought on the left in the Somme battle and won the victory of the Ancre in November 1916, when 5,000 German prisoners were taken.

To date I have been unable to establish if any men from the Border Regiment ever received any form of recognition in the way of awards or honours. Perhaps Captain Welsh also felt that his men never got the proper recognition they deserved.
In January 1924 he felt strongly enough to write to the War Office, sadly his letter no longer exists but the following answer was sent in reply.

Confidential

27340/10 (M.S.C.R) 17th January 1924.

Sir,

With further reference to your letter dated 3rd January 1924, I am directed to inform you that the records in the Department show your services to have been satisfactory and nothing of an adverse nature is recorded against you.

The following is a statement of your Services:-

Appointed to a temporary commission
as Second Lieutenant, The Border Regiment from Edinburgh University Officers' Training Corps.....................1.9.1914.
Promoted to temporary Lieutenant.....................31.12.1914.
Wounded at Suvla Bay. Gallipoli..................... 9.8.1915.
Appointed acting Captain...........................1.8.1916.
Relinquished the acting rank of Captain..............2.3.1919.

Captain W.A.Welsh,
14 Henderson Row,
Edinburgh

Officer's Statements

Following their release from captivity all officers were required to make written statements detailing the circumstances which led to their capture.

Any further communication on this subject
Should be addressed to___
The Secretary,
War Office
London, S.W.1,
And the following number quoted.

WAR OFFICE,
LONDON, S.W.1,
23 January 1919

27340/8
(A.G.3) CONFIDENTIAL

Sir,

I am commanded by the Army Council to request that you will be good enough to forward direct to this Department, for the purpose of record, a statement in duplicate setting out the incidents which led to your capture by the enemy as a Prisoner of War.

I am,

Sir,

Your obedient Servant,

R.V. Wade

23rd January 1919

CONFIDENTIAL

Captain William, Alexander, Welsh.
Commanding A Coy 11th Border Reg 97th Brig 32nd Division.

'On the morning of the 18th November 1916 the 97th Brigade in conjunction with other troops on both flanks were ordered to attack the enemy lines our objective being the second line trench.
At 6 am we attacked and everything went well, the first line being taken about 5 or 10 minutes after we started. After leaving some of the men detailed to mop up the front line profusely at work, I started off for the second line which was reached about 6.35am. By this time very few men were to be seen anywhere, in fact it was impossible to get in touch either on my right or left. About 6.45 I sent runners back to my commanding officer to give him full information as regards the situation. A short time afterwards the runners came back and said as they approached the German front line they had been fired on, consequently no information reached my CO. To make certain there were no mistakes I sent a wounded soldier back with six prisoners we had with us and sure enough he was also fired on, also-the result being he returned to us and the prisoners went back to their own trenches.
Our orders being we had to hold on at all costs, having managed to collect together about 70 men I started to prepare the place fit for defence, a dug-out was close at hand where we had about 40 wounded who were attended to by two or three of our men.
On the night of the 19th-20th and 21st patrols were sent out to try and get back to our lines to report the situation, but away to the front Germans holding this line were in exceptional

strength and they were unable to get through, by the night of the 22nd a patrol went out and got through as I afterwards heard.
Information been given by the patrol that got through that we cut off and unable to get back. Two attempts were made to relieve us on the 23rd-24th, but unfortunately both failed. From the 20th onwards the enemy made bombing raids etc daily but failed. Now having been in the enemy second line for eight and a half days the enemy attacked us with strong forces and we were compelled to surrender. In the end the main reason being our men were exhausted both from want of food and water for about eight days.
I have given you a full account of my capture. I was the senior officer there and I may say that anybody captured at the time as myself did his utmost to avoid been taken prisoner'.

In May of 1919 Captain Welsh was asked to submit the names of the other officers involved.

'In reply to your letter of the 21st inst, I am sorry I am unable to give the initials of one or two of the officers otherwise everything is in order'.

2nd Lieut D.W. Brady. 11th Border Regt.
2nd Lieut Lyon. 16th HLI.
2nd Lieut Scott. 16th HLI.
2nd Lieut Stewart. 16th HLI.
2nd Lieut Nixon. 11th Border Regt.

Captain. W.A. Welsh. 11th Border Regt

12th February 1919

CONFIDENTIAL

2nd Lieutenant John, Gilbert, Nixon.
B Coy 11th Border Regiment 97th Brig 32nd Division

'Sir I have the honour to report that I attacked on 18th November 1916, and immediately on arrival at my objective I reported to Captain Welsh 11th Border Regt, who took command of this particular sector. We got into communications with our troops on our left and right and everything seemed to be alright. After we had been in the position about one and a half hours a corporal came to me and informed me that the enemy had surrounded us and on looking over the parados I saw that we were completely surrounded and the enemy of course knew this.
I immediately informed Captain Welsh and we proceeded to collect bombs, but we only had about six left, so we decided to wait till night and discover by means of patrols what could be done, this took place about eight a.m. on the 18th Nov.
Accordingly the patrols went out and when they came back they reported what the enemy's position was very strongly held in every respect, and so we decided to wait till daybreak the next day to see if relief would come.
Day came and the enemy attacked us but we managed to drive him back, shortly afterwards one of our aeroplanes came over us and by means of flags we managed to inform him of our position, he returned shortly afterwards and signalled to us that we would be relieved at three pm on the 20th. The relief party endeavoured to get to us but it was a failure and exactly the same occurred on the 23rd Nov.

Somewhere about this date the enemy attacked us again and again we managed to drive him back and I think it was the same night that he tried to make a bombing attack which also was a failure for him. I might state that during this time I had nothing to eat or drink except shell water, and several men had died from wounds, dysentery and exhaustion.
Finally on the 26th Nov after being surrounded for eight and a half days the enemy attacked again in very superior numbers and owing to the majority of the bolts on the rifles refusing to open and lack of ammunition and starvation we were forced to surrender.
Our total strength was about eighty of which numbers nearly 50% were wounded and of no use for fighting.
A lance corporal had to try three times by himself before he could get back'.

I have the Honour to Be

Sir,

Your obedient Servant

J.G. Nixon
2/Lt
XI Border Regt

2nd January 1919

<u>CONFIDENTIAL</u>

2nd Lieutenant Malcolm, Murray Lyon
C Coy 16th Highland Light Infantry 97th Brig 32nd Division

'We attacked on the morning of November 18th 1916 the purpose being to capture the German first and second lines. I reached the second line with my platoon, but no forces came up on our right or left, and the Germans regained possession of their front line.
About midday of the same day we discovered we were surrounded and dug ourselves in, throughout the day stragglers and wounded came into us and the wounded were put in the dug-out.
Each night patrols went out but reported that it was impossible to get through the German lines unless we left our wounded (now numbering 60). In view of this and the shortage of bombs and the very slight chance of any of us getting through if we did by a rush, we decided to hold and wait for relief.
Of the six officers only three of us were able to do duty, and one of these Lieutenant Stewart 16th HLI was captured on the third night. The others either being wounded or suffering from shell shock and had to remain in the dug-out.
The Germans attacked us each day but were driven off, largely owing to the devotion to duty of our men, Lewis Gunners all of whom were killed or wounded before the end.
On the fifth day the Brigade attempted to relieve us but was unable to penetrate the German lines. Meanwhile our food and water supply ran out and it was difficult to keep the

seriously wounded alive. The Germans continued to attack us unsuccessfully and we took about 15 prisoners.
On the eighth afternoon (Nov26th 1916) the sentries were overcome before they could raise the alarm, the dug-out was bombed and we were taken prisoner'.

Malcom. M .Lyon.
Lieut. 3/att16/Highland Light Inf.

CONFIDENTIAL 23/3/19

2nd Lieutenant Frank Scott
C Coy 16th Highland Light Infantry 97th Brig 32nd Division

'The16th Highland Light Infantry attacked the German trench System known as the Munich (1st line) and Frankfort (2nd line) Trenches south of Serre on 18/11/16. Being in the first waves my objectives was Frankfort Trench; I reached my objective shortly after zero hour and consolidated. The remaining three waves failed to capture the front line through lack of reserves as that I was cut off, although surrounded 120 of us consisting of men from the 11th Border Regiment and 16th HLI managed to beat off several enemy attacks and hold our position for eight days, but ultimately had to capitulate owing to lack of ammunition, food and water, there were 3 Border officers and 2 HLI officers with us'.

F. Scott.
Lieutenant. 3rd HLI.

8 September 1918

CONFIDENTIAL

2nd Lieutenant Arthur Rylatt
C Coy 2nd Kings Own Yorkshire Light Infantry 97th Brig 32nd Division

'The attack took place at 6.10am on the 18th Nov 1916. Our objective was the third line of the Germans. Before I reached the second line I was severely wounded by shrapnel just below the elbow on the right arm, having bandaged this up I continued advancing for about 5 or 10 minutes when I was shot in the right forearm, the bullet fractured the bones.
I was taken to a dug-out in the second line where I found 60 to 100 men and 6 officers, all English there my wounds were attended to as well as possible.
This trench was held by the English, the senior officer sent some prisoners back in the charge of some men but the later returned reporting that we were cut off. The first line over which we had passed over was again held by Germans very much stronger. This happened on the 18th the first day of the attack. I was in too bad a condition to take any active part.
Our food rations lasted 3 days after which we had nothing whatsoever. Several attempts were made by Germans to reach us but they were every time unsuccessful owing to our rifle and Lewis gun fire, we asked for volunteers to try to break through the first line and though several fine fellows attempted, to my knowledge no one succeeded.
We then decided to attract the attention of an aeroplane as we had signaller with us. On the 6th day after several attempts he was successful signalling to the observer our condition and asked him to return and report, this happened on the

morning of the 6th day. The aeroplane flew back and returning half an hour later signalling that a rescue party Was being organised, about 4 o'clock in the afternoon we had a splendid barrage and I knew the relief were attacking. After waiting 2 to 3 hours nothing further happened and I had to conclude that the attack was a failure.
Our condition by this time was very bad, lack of food and water causing deaths amongst the wounded. On the 8th day an Englishman entered our dug-out and being asked where he had come from he replied that he had been sent by the Germans in the first line who had captured him in the relief attack, to ask us to surrender if we did we would be treated well. We kept this man with us and deciding not to surrender, the climax eventually came about when the Germans managed to reach us and threw a bomb down the staircase which threw us into a panic, our nerves being exceedingly raw after 5 days without food and having to drink rain water that we managed to collect out of shell holes.
We therefore had no alternative but to surrender, our condition was as bad as could be. My severe wounds were terrible, there we were captured and I was the only wounded officer out of the 7, I was taken alone to the nearest clearing station. I forgot to mention that we had nearly a dozen German prisoners in the dug-out the whole 8 days'.

Arthur. Rylatt. Lieut.
K.O.Y.L.I.

<u>CONFIDENTIAL</u>

Reference 115144/5 11th June 1919.

STATEMENT regarding circumstances which led to capture:-

'On Monday 18th the 96th Brigade attacked the German First and second line trenches. The 14th Brigade was protecting the left flank.
Both objectives were taken but the first one was retaken by the German bombing attack from the left flank. On the battalion right neither objectives were taken. The party in the second objective was then surrounded. I was with this party.
On November 21st previous attempts having failed, I attempted to pass from our position through the German line to arrange a combined attack and retirement.
Owing to our having about 50 wounded and the German line being strongly held, outside assistance was necessary to accomplish such a movement.
On the morning of the 22nd whilst continuing this attempt I was captured by a sentry group in the German first line'.

John Stewart
Lt. Spec. Reserve
H.L.I.

To The Secretary, War Office, **26th Jan 1919.**
Whitehall, London, S.W.1.

The Englishman's Nest

In October 1918 Lieutenant D.A.Scott 2nd Bn King's Own Yorkshire Light Infantry submitted a report to the War Office detailing his part in the action on Redan ridge. In his report he makes reference to the incident involving a party of men being cut off behind enemy lines and the unsuccessful attempts to rescue them.

Headquarters
97th. Infantry Brigade.

Herewith report as requested:-

'I know that on the night of the 21st and 22nd a party under a sergeant of the Borders went up and tried to get in touch with the isolated garrison, but was unsuccessful. On the 23rd it was decided that the 96th Brigade should attack and try to gain the trench where these men were. The attack was carried out, but it met with no success and the casualties were very heavy. After that nothing further was heard for some time until it came through the Corps Intelligence that the particular trench had been called by the German's 'The Englishman's Nest' on account of the way these men held out for about a week'.

8th. October 1918.

D.A. Scott. Lieutenant 2nd K.O.Y.L.I.[17]

---

[17] All the above Statements and reports made by officers who took part were obtained from The National archive Kew.

Two sides to every story, the German version

There remains one remarkable incident; one which really typified the end of this long battle.

During these days a noticeably large number of men carrying rations disappeared, so the men up front, who were suffering badly from wet conditions, had to go without food.

The whereabouts of these people was a mystery, and then a rumour started up that they had been grabbed by the Tommies during the pitch black night as they made their way forward. It was said that a thousand Tommies had broken through and that they were occupying a section of trench. Reconnaissance then showed that there was a nest of Tommies between the First and Second Positions, which also explained the endlessly circling British aircraft over one section of trench.

The Tommies had to be ejected immediately by means of a night operation. One battalion received the corresponding orders but, under the direction of a guide who apparently knew the area, they stumbled around for eight hours during a rainy night, until eventually the unlucky *Gefreiter* (corporal) broke down in tears, declaring that he had no idea where he was. As dawn broke it became clear that the whole group had gone round in circles and had arrived back at their starting point.

Now the capture of the Tommies was carefully planned and prepared for the next night but one when two complete battalions would be used.

Completely surrounded the enemy surrendered before even a hand grenade battle was necessary. There was a captain, three officers and 110 other ranks. They had hung on for eight long days, eating only food they had taken from our ration carriers. At the end of their struggle they wearily dragged themselves past us and into captivity. [18]

---

[18] The above account was taken from the history of 'Das Koeniglich Preussische reserve Infanterie Regiment Nr 15' pp386-387

We watched them not without high regard, towards the end the iron willed captain had apparently only prevented them from deserting by threatening them with his revolver.
The entire affair was marked by confusion on both sides. One prisoner stated that his colonel had said before the attack, 'This is the final effort! Make sure that you capture some ground and that's it for the year!' in fact the battle was extinguished like a burnt out volcano which had spewed out its last lava. The expenditure of strength in the mud and the cold was too great. Sickness and the reached significant proportions their drive and the troops lost their drive.

Another German version of events

The following account was taken from Hans Freiherrs book Somme published in 1937.

This report by the 169th can be expanded by a sensational episode. As related in the history of RIR 15, a party of British soldiers, comprising a captain, three officers and 110 men, which had broken through, held out as long as eight days between the German First and Second positions, without initially being noticed or even disturbed. The German regiment first became aware that something was awry because despite the heavy but normal amount of artillery fire this alone could not account for the noticeably large number of men carrying rations forward who were disappearing. Nobody could explain it, and then a rumour began about British troops which had broken through and were located somewhere in the intervening area.
It was decided in view of the continuing loss of ration carriers to get to the bottom of this strange situation, because over a protracted period, the constant cold, wet conditions meant that it was unacceptable for troops to have to hang on with

insufficient food and drink. Patrols were sent out and one of them was lucky enough to discover a nest of Tommies behind the lines, in a place where they must have been for some time. Now it was realised why British aircraft had been spending protracted periods circling above a particular section of trench. The commanders decided to deal with the nest. An initial attempt failed because it was not possible to find the British on a foggy night. Finally two entire battalions were deployed against the enemy which had infiltrated the position and they succeeded in disarming the little group which had broken in, without having to fight a serious battle.

Artist's impression of a British officer's defiant stand

The British were completely exhausted and starving.
Apart from the food they had been able to capture from the few German ration carriers, they had been completely without rations. The performance of the iron-willed commander of this band of men was all the more remarkable.
He was a British captain who, revolver in hand had forced his men to hang on until this surrender was forced on him, always in the uncertain hope that a fresh British attack would perhaps bring relief.
This minor incident is really symbolic of the battle itself at this time. Enemy attacks were no longer decided upon by daring decisions; instead, born out of near stalemate, they sought to take what could be taken.
The assaulting troops were not sacrificing themselves in the pursuit of victory; rather they were being sacrificed, because their commanders could not bring themselves to accept that the battle, with its rapidly disappearing returns, was not going to serve any external purpose, or achieve its strategic aims.
It was now suffocating in mud and despair.
Indicative of this was a statement of one of the many prisoners of war which was passed on by RIR 15.
According to this, the colonel of a British regiment had called out to his men at the end of a long inspiring address before the assault of 13th November,
'This is the final attack! See to it that you capture some ground and that's it for the year'.

This account was written in 1937 and the ease with which the battle was concluded according to this version of events may have been influenced by the German National Socialists Party who it is claimed often changed or tweaked events to strengthen the resolve of the Wehrmacht (Army)

The Men of Hereford

With the passage of time it is not possible to know if any of the transferees from the Herefordshire Regiment actually took part in the last stand in Frankfort Trench. What is known is that out of the one hundred and forty one men of the Lonsdales who perished in-between the period of 18th – 25th November 1916, sixty were ex-Herefords. [19]

The following accounts have been compiled from photographs and information gathered from surviving relatives of the men and local newspaper reports of the time.

It is know that several ex-Herefords were taken prisoner on the 18th November 1916 the day of the assault on Redan Ridge. The majority would have possibly suffered some sort of wound resulting in their capture. The following personal account is that of Sergeant Charles William Davies, who spent two years as a guest of the Kaiser in a German prisoner of war camp.

'I was captured at Beaumont-Hamel on the 18th of November 1916. I was buried by a shell and rendered unconscious, and when I came to I found I was in a German dugout. I was slightly wounded by a piece of shrapnel in my right knee, but this did not prevent me walking, as the shrapnel was just under the skin I was able to get it out myself with a knife. We were marched to Cambrai. On the last part of the march a man died of exhaustion but the guard simply pulled him off the road and put a sentry over him, we were prevented from taking his body with us'.

From the 21st November 1916 to the 8th December 1916 Sgt Davies was held at a collecting station for prisoners in Cambrai know as the 'Citadel'.

---

[19] In total 141 Lonsdales lost their lives in-between 18-25th Nov 1916 this figure includes those who died of wounds, many as a result of the action on the 18th.
The 16th HLI figures for the same period were 163 casualties.

'We were put in a room above a stable; we lost all idea of time as the windows were blocked out with boards and we could not tell whether it was daytime or night.
The crowding in the room in which we were placed was absolutely cruel, you could not move around without treading upon somebody, and there was no ventilation. There were no washing or sanitary arrangements provided beyond four great tubs in the room which the prisoners cleared each morning'.

During his time at the Citadel, Sgt Davies contracted dysentery, but it was only following the intervention of the local Priest that ensured that Sgt Davies was eventually moved to the local hospital for treatment. Here he remained until the 22nd December, when due to a slight improvement in his condition he was again moved to the Marien Hospital at Aachen. On the 11th January 1917 he was considered fit to be discharged from hospital and was taken under armed guard by train to Friedrichsfeld prisoner of war camp in Wesel, Westphalia, Germany. Here he would remain a prisoner until he eventually made his escape on the 7th of January 1918.

'We were lodged here in wooden huts, the majority of the huts were good but some let the wet through the roofs. They were well ventilated and had windows and skylights and at night were lighted by electric light. Within the huts were stoves for heating which at night we used to bank up with coke but they went out in the night and the huts were very cold first thing in the morning in the winter. There were good arrangements for washing and we had two days a week on which we could go to the baths, these were hot shower baths'. I was employed as a supervisor in the packet office but the majority of the prisoners were out on working parties at farms, mines, munitions factories and zinc factories. The men on the working parties received 30 Pfennig's per day'.

Compared to the prisoner of war camps of World War two it would appear that the men enjoyed certain privileges.

'There was a canteen in the camp which was a very dear one, I never bought anything so I cannot give the prices, but the following articles could be obtained there; - clocks, watchers, chains, safety razors, small souvenir knifes, hair brushers and combs, pipes, cigarettes, cigars, matches, games such as draughts, dominoes, cards, German beer, lemonade, sometimes onions one mark for 50 kilos, sometimes cauliflower. Writing materials, pencils, ink, pens, letter paper and postcards and German newspapers. We could get what they called wine from at another department of the canteen; this was about half a pint for one mark 20 Pfennig's.

I do not know, personally anything of the food supplied by the Germans beyond that is not fit to eat and that we had our Red-Cross food parcels, so we gave it to the Russian prisoners. During the summer months instead of bread we received biscuits from Switzerland, but these are not satisfactory, as they are so hard that we cannot eat them. We used to soak them in a bucket of water but when they were dry again they became very hard, and considerable force was required to break them. The biscuits were harder than dog biscuits, we used to crack them with a hammer and make fish cakes, puddings and other things with the crumbs'.

British prisoners of war working in camp post-office[20]

[20] Sgt Davies was employed as a postman at Chepstow in Monmouthshire before he joined the army.

British and French POWs standing in line (Author's collection)

POW camp in Germany showing typical layout of barracks (Author's collection)

Clothing was very hard to source and the prisoners were occasionally offered an opportunity to exchange bits and pieces of uniform. Most refused to swap considering the replacement items to be of very poor quality, certain garments having been manufactured from paper which soon fell to pieces.

Letters and parcels from home were received on a regular basis but were always opened by the German censors; the majority of the prisoners were convinced that items of food were stolen from their food parcels by the camp guards.

Harsh treatment could be expected for prisoners who disobeyed the rules.

'I saw no cases of cruelty, either to the British prisoners or those of any other nationality. Although I was never on working parties I believe that the treatment of prisoners on commandos were very brutal, I have seen men come back in shocking states after being on a working party. I have seen great scars on them, on their heads and bodies, also men with broken arms and legs and these have told me that their injuries were caused by the Germans, both soldiers and civilians. These cruelties were perpetrated because it was alleged that the prisoners, refused to work, or did not work well enough to please the civilians who were employing the prisoners by contract from the Government.

The Germans sometimes used Indian-rubber truncheons, a little over a foot long with which they hit a man over the head. This will knock a man senseless without leaving a scar. In the coalmines they hit the prisoners over the head with their safety lamps. Men do not mind working on farms, but I have seen men who have been put to work on munitions come back to camp with their fingers crushed which they had themselves done purposely so as to make themselves unfit for this work. We were to count any German subject our superior, whether we were officers, NCOs or other ranks. For striking a German in the presence of assembled troops, we were liable to be shot. Failure to salute an officer or NCO was punished with fourteen days imprisonment. Attempting to escape or if you had anything with you to aid escape fourteen days imprisonment'.

At the beginning of 1917 Sgt Davies recalls several other men of the 11th Border Regiment being brought into the camp.

'At the beginning of 1917 I spoke to several men from my own battalion who the Germans had kept behind their front lines they had been employed cutting trees, and had been under our own shell fire. They were half starved and in a terrible condition, we collected bread for them but their hunger was so great that they could not help raiding us and fighting for it. It was terrible to see them'.

As the war dragged on conditions in Germany started to worsen with food shortages, which in turn led to riots amongst the civil population. Sgt Davies noticed several changes.

'In 1917 I was told by one of the censors that there were riots in all the towns around the camp over the food question and the censors were to go down and act as guards during the weekend while they were not employed in the camp. On one occasion one of the censors named Langerkampf started crying and told me that in Dusseldorf machine guns had been used to quiet the crowds and that his wife had been amongst the crowd but that she was safe'. He told me that if he had to go that he would not use a machine gun but when he returned the following Monday he said that he had been obliged to do so'. The men employed as guards at the camp were old men, that is men over fifty and boys of about seventeen, some were obviously wounded and only armed with a revolver whilst others were armed with rifle and bayonet'.

On the 7th of January 1918 Sgt. Davies made his escape from Germany he gives little detail of the events other than to say.

'The country through which I passed while making my escape appeared to be deserted, and only about one field out of twenty was ploughed up. We only saw one man and he was trimming hedges. There was no snow on the ground at the time and nothing to prevent working. It was fine weather for ploughing'.

Following Sgt. Davies safe return to England he was formally interviewed and made a full statement regarding his treatment as a prisoner of war to a solicitor. [21]

Opinion of examiner.

'I examined Sergeant Charles William Davies today at 53 Coleman Street E.C.2. He appeared to me to be a good witness and gave answers to the questions put to him clearly and intelligently.
He gave the information contained in the report readily, and so far as I am able to judge, very fairly, and without exaggeration.
Except as to his treatment while on the march to Cambrai, and at the Citadel in that town, he has very few complaints to make of his own treatment as a prisoner of war, but he spoke strongly of that received by those sent on working parties, and those who had been working behind the lines on the Western front.
In my opinion the witness has given an honest and straightforward account of his life as a prisoner of war and one which may, so far as his personal knowledge extends, be accepted as thoroughly reliable'. Dated the 26th day of January 1918.

Sgt Davies returned safely to Hereford and was reunited with his family at his home 7 Mostyn Street, Whitecross, Hereford. In recognition of his brave conduct whilst escaping from captivity as a POW he was awarded the Military Medal for bravery in the field.

Another ex–Hereford who was taken prisoner during the attack on Redan Ridge on the 18th November 1916 was Private W. King. He had originally served with the 1/1st Bn of the Herefords and took part in the Suvla Bay landings in the Gallipoli campaign of 1915. Over an eighteen week period hundreds of men from the Herefords became casualties many

---

[21] Statement recorded 26th January 1918 by R C Swaine Solicitor 53 Coleman St, London. Narrative of Sgt Davies statement taken from Public Records Office Reference WO/161/99

suffering not only wounds but enteric fever and even frostbite. At some point in the campaign Pte King returned as a casualty to England, following his recovery he was transferred to the Lonsdales but soon found himself back on active service this time in France. Following his capture he was taken to Germany where he remained until the end of the war. Upon his return to England he was reunited with his family and lived in Rotherwas, Hereford. Sadly, he died of tuberculosis in 1932 and is buried in St Martin's Church, Hereford.

Pte.W. King. (Picture kindly donated by Mr King (son) Hereford)

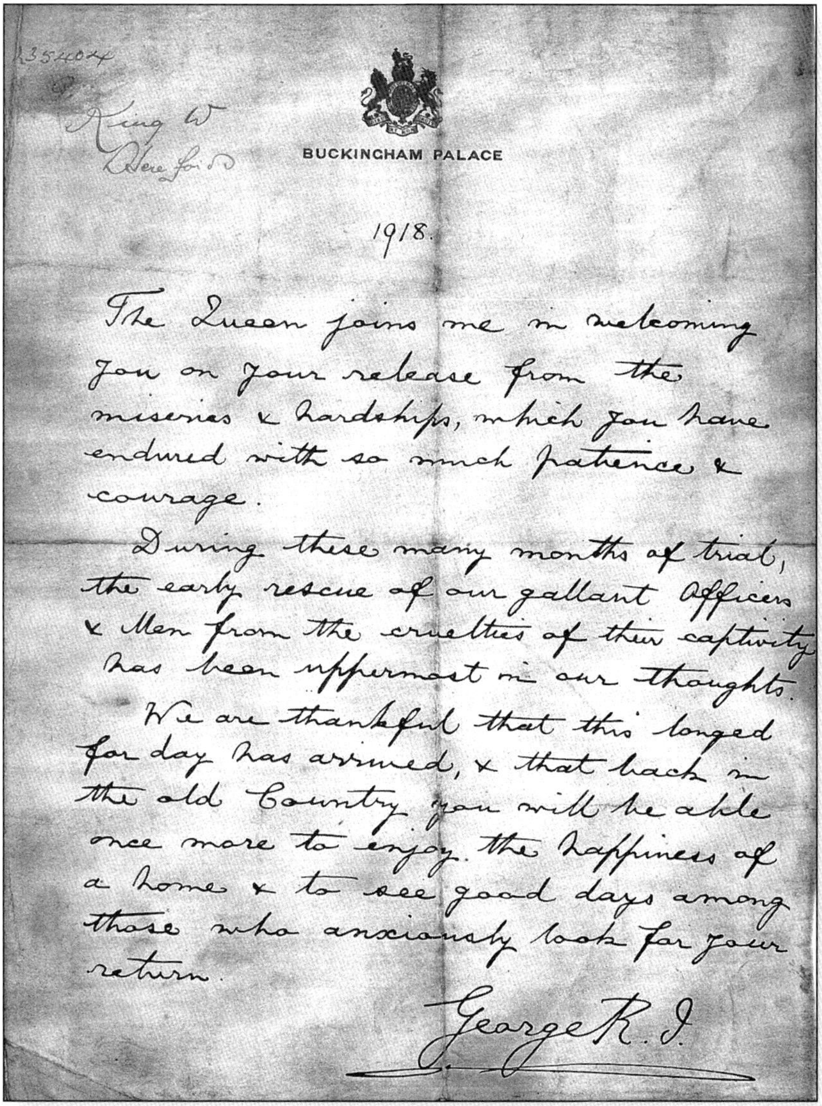

354024
King W
Hereford

BUCKINGHAM PALACE

1918.

The Queen joins me in welcoming you on your release from the miseries & hardships, which you have endured with so much patience & courage.

During these many months of trial, the early rescue of our gallant Officers & Men from the cruelties of their captivity has been uppermost in our thoughts.

We are thankful that this longed for day has arrived, & that back in the old Country you will be able once more to enjoy the happiness of a home & to see good days among those who anxiously look for your return.

George R.I.

Copy of a printed letter sent by King George V to prisoners upon their return to UK (Author's collection note Pte King's details top left corner)

Private Harry Price Herefordshire Regiment
(Kindly donated by his family)

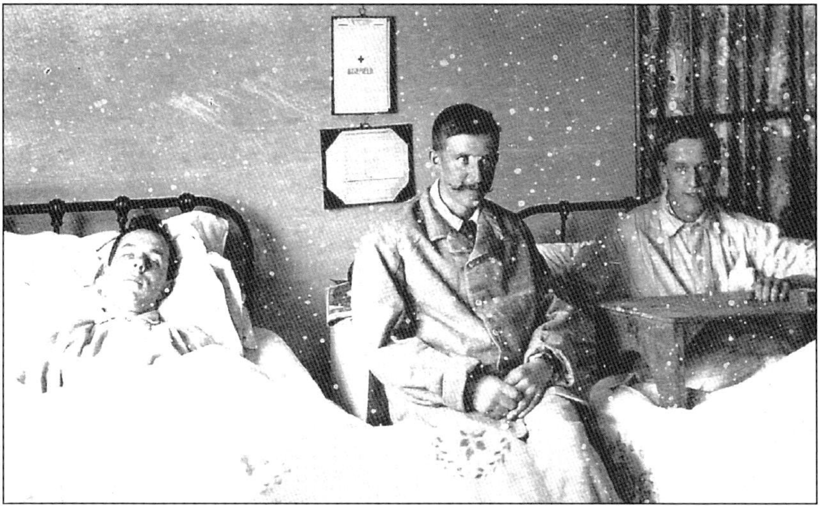

Pte. Harry Price centre in hospital 1916-17
(Kindly donated by his family)

Pte 27687 Harry Price served with D company 11th Bn Border Regiment; he landed in France on the 1st of October 1916 and joined the Lonsdales on the 11th of October. During the action to capture Redan Ridge he received a gunshot wound to his chest.
Sometime after the 8th March 1917 he was evacuated back to England to convalesce at the National Sanatorium in Benenden Kent. As a result of his injuries Harry never returned to the front and was eventually discharged in August 1917 being unfit for further military service. Following the war Harry moved back to Lydbrook near Ross-On-Wye. He went on to have ten children and even married for a second time aged 90.

Harry Price in 1976 aged 90 and his second wife on their wedding day
(kindly donated by his family)

LOCAL NEWS REPORTS

Many of the men who took part in the attack on the 18th of November 1916 were wounded and several good accounts of their experiences exist. Some survivors when fully recovered returned to France in some cases only to suffer more wounds or even death. The following extracts have been taken from the Leominster News as published in 1916, a local newspaper now long gone.

HEREFORDS IN ACTION

Mr and Mrs W Lewis 38 Ryelands Road Leominster have received a letter from their son Pte. A Lewis 11th Border Regiment stating that he has been wounded and is in hospital in Manchester, in his letter he says.

' The bullet went right through my right thigh and out the other side, we got to the hospital on Tuesday night (21st November) I can think myself lucky to get off with this as I expect you will hear of a lot being killed. I expect there will be a lot of my mates who came out with the Herefords with me gone under. It was Saturday morning the 18th when we went over and we had a hot time waiting at the other end when we got there'.

Pte. A. Lewis first joined 'Kitchener's Army' in August 1914, and served in the 5th South Wales Borderers Regt, being discharged last March unfit for service. He again enlisted joining the 3/1st Herefordshire Regt, and went to France in September attached to the 11th Border Regt.

LOCAL NEWS REPORTS

Pte Lewis appears to have made a full recovery and returned to duty in March 1917 only to be wounded a second time.

LEOMINSTER BOMBER BAYONETED

Mr and Mrs W. Lewis, 38 Ryelands Road Leominster, have been officially notified that their son, Pte Alec Lewis Border Regt was wounded on July 14th and was in hospital at Rouen with a bayonet wound in the back. Pte Lewis is a bomber and was engaged in a raid when he was wounded. Writing from a VAD hospital at Tiverton, Devon he states that he landed in England on Wednesday of last week and is doing well. This is the second time Pte Lewis has been wounded. He was shot through the right hip on November the 18th 1916, and was sent to England. He returned to the front again last March, and states he has seen some rough times again.

DIED OF WOUNDS IN FRANCE

It is with regret that we announce the death from wounds received in action in France of Pte. Harry Wilkins. 11th Border Reg, only son of Mrs Wilkins 122 South Street Leominster. On Friday last Mrs Wilkins received a communication from the chaplain stating that her son was wounded and had laid out in the snow for many hours before being brought in. This was followed by an official wire on Saturday to the effect that Pte. Wilkins was dangerously ill in hospital in France, wounded in the left arm. On Tuesday morning two letters were received. The Rev R.C. Jones, wrote,

'Your son Pte H Wilkins of the 11th Border Reg is lying in A 5 ward hospital X I General Hospital France. He was wounded in the left shoulder and is feeling better after the operation yesterday. Will you write him a cheerful letter? It will do him good'.

The Matron after saying that Pte Wilkins was in a dangerous condition wrote;

'He had an operation yesterday to try to improve it and it is impossible to say what will be the result. He is having every possible care and attention and has all he wants, so you must hope for the best.

On Tuesday night however, a further official wire intimated that Pte. Wilkins died on November 27th. The following day a post card was received from the Matron dated November 26th;

'Your son is much worse I am sorry to tell you, and the surgeon thinks there is practically no chance of his recovery. He is very peaceful'.

Before enlisting in the Hereford Regiment on February the 8th Private Harry Wilkins was employed as a baker at Ashperton, Ledbury. He left Leominster three years ago, being previously engaged with Mr Pointer, Etnam Street. Pte Wilkins was only 24 years of age, was much liked and deep sympathy is felt with the bereaved mother.

Pte. H. Wilkins. Buried in Etapes France.

LOCAL NEWS REPORTS

KINGTON MEN MISSING

Information has been received by his parents, Mr and Mrs Cowdell of Woodbrook, Kington, that their son Pte. Arthur. S. Cowdell 3/1st Herefordshire Reg, attached to the Border Reg is 'missing'. He joined the Herefords some months ago and was recently sent to France.

Unofficial information contained in a letter sent to Titley from a soldier serving in the same regiment states that Pte Cuthbert Flowers of the 3/1st HFDs, attached to the Border Reg is also 'missing' previous to joining up when his group was called Pte Flowers had been for several years in the employ of Mr. J .M. Curre. Master of the Radnorshire and West Herefordshire Hunt, as stud groom second whip, and resided at The Kennels Titley, he married since joining the Army.

Pte. Cowdell had in fact been killed in action on the 18th of November, eventually his body was recovered from the battlefield and he is now buried in Wagon Road Cemetery. As to the fate of Pte Flowers he is not listed as a casualty and presumably survived the war it is possible that he may have been taken prisoner.

Private Arthur Cowdell seated with unknown friend (picture kindly donated by Pte Cowdell's family from Hereford)

LEDBURY SOLDIERS MISSING

Official notification has been received that three Ledbury men, Pte Frank Tarbath, David Owen, and E Williams of the Border Reg are missing. Pte Tarbath is the youngest son of Mr Harry Tarbath Seven Stars Inn Ledbury, and is a single man. He enlisted under the group system in the Herefordshire Reg and was later transferred to the Border Reg, and has been in the Ancre battle. Pte Owen is a married man with two children and was formerly employed by Mr C Hill, sculptor, New Street. He was a member of the National Reserve having done several years service in the Territorials, and was called up in September 1914 going into the 2/1st HFDs and was this year transferred to the 3rd Bn at Oswestry, and subsequently the Border Reg.
Pte Ted Williams is a married man with three children and enlisted in the autumn of 1914, in the 2nd HFDs subsequently being transferred to the 3rd Bn and then the Border Reg. In civil life he worked as a gardener for Dr Miles Wood Orchardleigh.

All three men went out with a draft for the Border Reg. Two other Ledbury men of the draft Privates W P Clarke and W Davis are wounded and in hospital in England.

MISSING MAN PRESUMED KILLED

The long silence regarding the fate of Private Frank. G. Tarbath, Seven Stars Inn. Ledbury has at last been broken, and he is now presumed to have been killed about November18th last year, from which date he was originally reported missing. Private Tarbath joined up under the groups system in the early days of 1916 at Oswestry, and proved himself a very smart soldier. He was later drafted to the Border Reg, with a number of other local soldiers.

The body of Francis Tarbath was never found and like numerous others from the 11th Bn Border Reg his name is recorded on the Thiepval Memorial to the Missing on the Somme. In total twenty nine former members of the Hereford Regiment listed as serving with the 11th Border Regiment at the time of their deaths are recorded on the memorial which is dedicated to men whose bodies were lost or never identified and have no known grave.

Private Ted Williams had in fact been taken prisoner and is not listed as a casualty and is presumed to have returned safely to England at the end of the war in 1918.

Pte Francis Tarbath (right of picture) and his brother Henry Mathew Tarbath (left) (Picture kindly donated by Mr John Rawlins, Ledbury)

No further news regarding Pte. David Owen appears to have been published in the local press; however he was in fact killed in action sometime on the 18th or 19th of November 1916 during the attack on Redan Ridge.

During the attack it is believed that a number of men from various different regiments did in fact cross over into each others sectors. Now separated from their battalions these men grouped together to form mixed units. On the extreme left flank of the attack one such band of Tommies managed to advance deep into enemy territory into a trench system know as Ten Tree Alley towards the village of Serre. There, like the defenders holding out in Frankfort Trench, they found themselves cut off and isolated.

Constantly under attack by the enemy the men held out until there supply of ammunition was exhausted. Out numbered and with no supplies the men were soon over-run and the small band completely wiped out. [22]Unconfirmed reports made the following day by a survivor of the Redan Ridge attack claimed that he had seen a group of around forty men who appeared determined to hold out. However, he was uncertain of their exact position, but later a similar number of bodies were discovered fuelling speculation that this was indeed the same group previously reported by the survivor.

What is known is that the 11th Borderers have the largest number of graves within Ten Tree Alley Cemetery, bearing the date 18/11/16. The cemetery is situated close to the area where the men fought and died, David Owen and three other Hereford Lonsdales are amongst the Borderers within the cemetery.

Perhaps they may have been amongst the defenders of the trench.

---

[22] Neither reports as to sightings of a group of up to 40 men fighting or subsequent numbers of bodies being discovered can be confirmed in any of the official reports or diaries that the Author has had access to whilst compiling this book.

Pte D E Owen (picture kindly donated by Mrs B Hill Ledbury)

David E Owen was in fact not a native of Herefordshire; he was born 20th September 1881 in Betws-y-Coed in Wales. In the early 1900's he moved to Ledbury and took up employment with Hatton Builders as a Stone Mason. A talented man he was said to be a great singer an artist and a wood carver. And it is reputed that he carved the feathers on the sign to the front of the Feathers Hotel in Ledbury.

EDWARD NICHOLAS

Pte Edward Nicholas. Picture kindly donated by Mrs M Lancaster Hereford

20 year old Private Edward Nicholas son of Helen Nicholas of Swainshill, Herefordshire. Was taken prisoner having been wounded on the 18/11/16, he later died of his wounds on 15th December 1916 and is buried in Berlin South-Western Cemetery in Germany.

Some of the local men who served and died with the Lonsdales

Pte. HEBER SMITH,
Border Regiment. Killed in action in France, November 18th, 1916.

Pte. C. BEDELL,
Border Regiment. Killed in action in France, November 18th, 1916.

Pte. BERT HAINES,
11th Border Regt., died November 21st, 1916, from wounds received in action, in France, on the 18th. Son of Mr. and Mrs. George Haines, Marston, Pembridge.

Pte. C. E. HAYNES,
Border Regt., wounded and missing in France, October 26th, 1917, afterwards presumed to be dead. Son of Mr. C. Haynes, of Stretford.

Pte. J. P. SEAGER,
Border Regt., killed in action in France, in April, 1917. Youngest son of Mrs. Seager, 38, High Street, Leominster, and of the late Mr. William Seager.

L.-Cpl. G. T. BOUNDS,
Herefordshire Regt., killed in action on July 29th, in France. His parents live at The Moor, Bodenham.

Pte. T. BROOKES,
Border Regt., killed in action, in France, on Nov. 18th, 1916. Son of Mrs. E. Brookes, The Laure's, Leysters.

KNOWN UNTO GOD

Grave of an Unknown Soldier Author's collection 2005

'Known unto God', the simple inscription found on the head stone of an unknown soldier of the Border Regiment. When the battlefields were cleared it was not always possible due to the appalling carnage to identify individuals other than by the regiment. In lots of cases grieving relatives had no grave that they could visit and for some it held a distant hope that their son, brother or father may yet still be alive perhaps in one of the numerous hospitals and institutions caring for the thousands of sick and wounded. Scores of these men who due to the terrible experiences that they had suffered lost their minds trapped in a world full of horrors and torment.

Many years have now passed and no veterans of this conflict survive, but what does remain as a permanent reminder to the sacrifice made by the many thousands of men from all over the British Isles are the cemeteries and memorials maintained and cared for by the Commonwealth War Graves Commission. Their tireless work ensures that every soul from a general to a private receives the best attention that the Commission gardeners and workers can provide. Over the next few pages are some of the cemeteries which contain the graves of Hereford Lonsdales on the Somme, many hundreds of miles from home these sons of the county of Herefordshire now in peace where they fought and died so that we may live free.

The Silent Cities

Thiepval Memorial (Author's collection)

Thiepval Memorial to the Missing on the Somme records the names of 73,357 men whose bodies were lost.
Designed by Sir Edwin Lutyens a leading architect of the time, his other works include the Cenotaph in London. Construction began in 1929 and was finally completed in 1931. The Memorial was officially inaugurated in 1932 by the Prince of Wales.
Twenty nine Hereford Lonsdales are recorded on the memorial. Their names can be found on Pier and Face 6A and 7C.

**HERE ARE RECORDED
NAMES OF OFFICERS
AND MEN OF THE
BRITISH ARMIES WHO
FELL
ON THE SOMME
BATTLEFIELDS
JULY 1915 FEBRUARY 1918
BUT TO WHOM
THE FORTUNE OF WAR
DENIED THE KNOWN
AND HONOURED BURIAL
GIVEN TO THERE
COMRADES IN DEATH**

Portland stone block set high into the monument reads (Author's collection)

To the front of the memorial is an Anglo-French Cemetery, to signify the joint efforts of both Britain and France in WWI. Both countries provided the remains of three hundred soldiers, the French placed to the right the British to the left just as they faced the Germans in 1916.

The Silent Cities

Wagon Road Cemetery contains 195 graves of which 49 are men of 11th Border Regiment, who took part in the attack on Redan Ridge on the 18th November 1916. Wagon Road Cemetery has the highest concentration of Hereford Lonsdales graves on the Somme, in total 20 of the 49 Border Regiment graves are those of men from Herefordshire. The grave of Lieutenant G.N.Higginson 16th Lancashire Fusiliers who led the last rescue attempt to relieve the isolated defenders of Frankfort Trench on the 23rd November 1916 can also be found within the cemetery.

Wagon Road Cemetery (Author's collection 2005)

The Silent Cities

Ten Tree Alley Cemetery contains sixty seven graves from three separate actions. Four of the graves are those of Hereford Lonsdales, these men penetrated even deeper into German held territory than their colleagues in Frankfort Trench. Similarly they became isolated and cut off, confronted by the enemy in overwhelming numbers they fought on until they had used up all their ammunition. Eventually they were overrun by the enemy and perished.

Ten Tree Alley Cemetery (Author's collection 2005)

Munich Trench Cemetery above (Author's collection 2005)
Frankfort Trench Cemetery below (Author's collection 2005)

The Silent Cities

Frankfort Trench Cemetery contains one hundred and thirty four graves, two of which are Hereford Lonsdales. Similarly, Munich Trench Cemetery contains one hundred and twenty six graves of which two are Hereford Lonsdales.

Serre Road No 1 Cemetery contains three graves of Hereford Lonsdales. As these graves are situated on the extreme left flank of the battlefield it is possible that the men took part in the attack at Ten Tree Alley, or that their bodies were recovered much later and placed in Serre Road No 1 Cemetery.

Serre Road No 1 Cemetery (Author's collection 2005)

The Silent Cities

Lonsdale Cemetery does not contain any of the Hereford Lonsdales; however it would be impossible to complete this section without paying tribute to the men from the battalion who lost their lives on the 1st July 1916.

Entrance to the Lonsdale Cemetery (Author's collection 2005)

Established in 1917 the cemetery originally contained ninety-six graves which now forms plot one, to be found just inside as you enter by the main gate. Later a large concentration of bodies was added, and the cemetery now contains one thousand five hundred and nineteen men.

More than half of the graves belong to unknown's soldiers.

The Grave of Sergeant. J .Y. Turnbull. V C. in Lonsdale Cemetery (Author's collection 2005)

James Turnbull served with the 17th Highland Light Infantry; he was killed on the 1st July 1916 on the opening day of the Battle of the Somme.

(Note the alternative spelling of Serjeant as used by some regiments)

Visiting the battlefields today

Visiting the battlefields and cemeteries on the Somme is now relatively easy and affordable. Both the operators of the Channel tunnel and Ferry Companies offer throughout the year various channel crossing deals and many bargain prices can be found by visiting the Internet.
Once in France it is only a moderate drive of approximately 1 to 1 ½ hrs on good and compared to the UK quiet motorway to get to the Somme-Region.

Mother-Nature is a great healer and the majority of the battle scared landscape has returned to its former rural splendour a mixture of rolling countryside and agriculture.
Well signposted, today's visitor will find the major sites and places of remembrance easy to find and easily accessible.
In many cases just behind one of the immaculately kept memorials and cemeteries may be a small cops' or wood where often can be found the remains of a former trench system or some other evidence of the long past conflict of WW1.

A word of warning. Always remember the land belongs to someone, the vast majority of French farmers and land owners respect the sacrifice made by the thousands of men from all nations who gave their lives to set France free, but in turn expect you not to trespass and damage crops or property. A courteous request to view or a little thought and consideration will in most cases result in a successful visit.
It is not an uncommon sight to see placed in the corner of a field or by the side of the road unexploded munitions shells, hand-grenades of various size and nationality. Every year the iron harvest yields tons of unexploded ordinance and relics of the war, which naturally make their way to the surface and are exposed by the ploughing of the fields.
Beware what may now appear to be a harmless looking rusting antique can still prove to be deadly and in many cases time has

not reduced its potential to harm but only made it more unstable and dangerous.
Never be tempted to pick up and inspect or consider just taking one home as a souvenir. Not only do you risk your life, but if caught by the authorities you will almost certainly face prosecution.
Stick to tracks and pathways, many hazards await those who foolishly wonder.

WHERE TO STAY

Depending on your personal preferences today's visitor can choose from camping to bed-breakfast accommodation to hotels. For the first visit many prefer to base themselves in one of the local towns such as Albert or Peronne. Here you will find a good selection of hotels and restaurants as well as shops and tourist information centres. If however you wish to sample rural living, numerous farms and village locations offer B&B accommodation at very reasonable rates.

GETTING AROUND

In the main most visitors will use the car, whilst this may prove to be the most effective way of travelling from A to B you may wish to consider taking with you a bicycle. This is an excellent way to view the battlefields, and often results in observing many sights which you would miss by driving past in a car.
Or by far the best method of getting around is to invest in a good pair of boots and simply walk. Also highly recommended is a set of waterproof clothing.

1st JULY TOUR

For those who wish to visit the route taken by the Lonsdales on the fateful morning of July 1st 1916, the following suggested tour might be considered. Allow yourself 3-4 hrs and read this route prior to starting ensuring that you are fully prepared.

An ideal starting point would be to park at the newly completed visitors centre at Thiepval. Here you will find good parking facilities and an excellent information centre. As well as a wealth of information regarding the battle, you will find internet access to both the Commonwealth war Graves Commission and Soldiers Died database.

The centre also contains toilets and a small drinks and snacks area which can be purchased from vending machines; you can also obtain books, maps and souvenirs from the centre shop.

START

After leaving the centre follow the path that leads to Thiepval Memorial to the missing on the Somme.

Thiepval Memorial (Author's collection 2005)

You may wish to spend some time exploring the memorial. Check the memorial registers found in the bronze cabinets set into the two columns. You could find a family member of yours recorded here. You can also view the pier containing the names of the Lonsdales.

When ready returns to the main path, but instead of returning to the visitor centre turn right and continue along the path. The gravel path will eventually change to a dirt track running between two fields, keep straight on. In the distance you will see on the horizon two clumps of trees; this is the sight of the *Granatloch*. This formed part of the German Leipzig Salient defences. This used to be the quarry for the village of Authuille. From here the enemy wreaked deadly machine gun fire on the advancing troops. Now overgrown it is hard to imagine that it was once an important German position.

Granatloch left of track (Author's collection 2005)

This is also close to the area where Sergeant James Turnbull 17th HLI won the Victoria Cross on the 1st July.
Carry on walking along the track until you reach the minor made road, over which the track continues. Stop here for a moment at the road. Straight ahead is the track along which the Lonsdales made their advance. Look left and you should see in the distance Lonsdale Cemetery. When ready turn left and walk along the road downhill heading towards the cemetery. Just before you reach the path that leads to the cemetery, stop and look up to the ridge on the left. This is the approximate location of the *Nordwerk;* from here the Germans fired deadly swathes of machine gun bullets at the advancing troops.

View from the road, with track leading into Authuille wood, from which the Lonsdales advanced (Author's collection 2005)

Follow the grass track which leads to Lonsdale Cemetery, just before you reach the entrance stop. If you look to your left you can follow the up hill track along which the Lonsdales advanced. When ready enter the cemetery, here you will find many of the 1st July casualties from the Borderers and the other Bns of the 97th Brigade.

Track leading to Lonsdale Cemetery (Author's collection 2005)

Take a moment to view the grave of Sergeant Turnbull V.C. his citation for the award reads.

'Although his party was wiped out and was replaced several times during the day, Sergeant Turnbull never wavered in his determination to hold the post, the loss of which would have been very serious. Almost single-handed, he maintained his position, and displayed the highest degree of valour and skill in the performance of his duties'.

When ready leave the cemetery and retrace your steps back up the road towards Thiepval. As you reach the track which leads back to the Granatloch stop. Now turn left and go along the track in the direction of Authuille wood. Behind you should be Thiepval memorial, to your left should be Lonsdale Cemetery and facing you should be Authuille wood.

Eventually you will see the now gated entrance leading into the wood. Stop and look around, this is the area from which the Lonsdales exited the wood only to be cut to pieces by German machine gun fire. Open the gate and enter the wood, please ensure you close the gate behind you. Take a moment to view the scene and let your eyes adjust to the slightly darker conditions in the wood.

The track and gated entrance to Authuille wood (Author's collection 2005)

As you walk down the track look left and right and you should see the remains of two trench systems, (left)

Chequerbent Street and (right) Chowbent Street. On the 1st July both trenches were crammed with wounded men desperately trying to make their way back to the field dressing stations. At the same time advancing troops were trying to make their way up the trenches to the starting off point. It is believed that due to the congestion the Lonsdales failed to use either trench systems, deciding instead to make their advance along the main track.

Just off the track the remains of trench system (Author's Collection 2005)

Continue down the track, note the many shell craters both left and right of the track. At the bottom of the track you should find another gated exit. Leave the wood via this gate again ensuring you close it behind you. As you continue down the track just to your left is the area where the Lonsdales waited prior to the start of their advance through the wood.

Shell craters in Authuille wood (Author's collection 2005)

Continue along the track which will eventually bear right. You should see to your right Blighty Valley Cemetery in the distance. Follow the track, which now starts to rise slightly and changers into a metalled road. Keep on until you run into another larger road, turn right and walk the few yards to Crucifix Corner.

Crucifix Corner (Author's collection 2005)

Crucifix Corner also known as Quarry Dugouts is situated at the cross-roads that leads to the villages of Authuille and Aveluy. (Take care you may encounter fast local traffic).

This was a very busy and important area during the Somme campaign. It was a main supply route and many thousands of troops including the Lonsdales passed through on their way to the frontline. To the rear of the crucifix just inside the wood are the remains of several trench systems. A little further along the Authuille road is the former quarry now used as a scrap yard, during 1916 it contained many dugouts and shelters cut into the soft chalk quarry face. On the 1st July 1916 the cross roads were jam-packed with hundreds of casualties on stretchers awaiting evacuation to one of the main base or field hospitals.

You now have the choice of either simply following the route back the way you have just come. Alternatively you can continue along the road that leads to Authuille. (Be aware of local traffic). On route to Authuille you can if you choose stop off and visit Blighty Valley Cemetery, which contains many graves from the 1st July battle. When you eventually arrive in the village of Authuille, time permitting you can also pay a visit to the small village cemetery, formerly used as a casualty clearing station in 1916.

Authuille Cemetery (Author's collection 2005)

Return to the main village road and continue until you see a road off to the right signposted Lonsdale Cemetery. Follow the road up hill, eventually it will bring you back to the track which leads to Thiepval Memorial. Whilst this is not a particularly difficult route, you should allow 3-4 hrs, and be sure you are comfortable with the route prior to attempting it.

Map not to scale

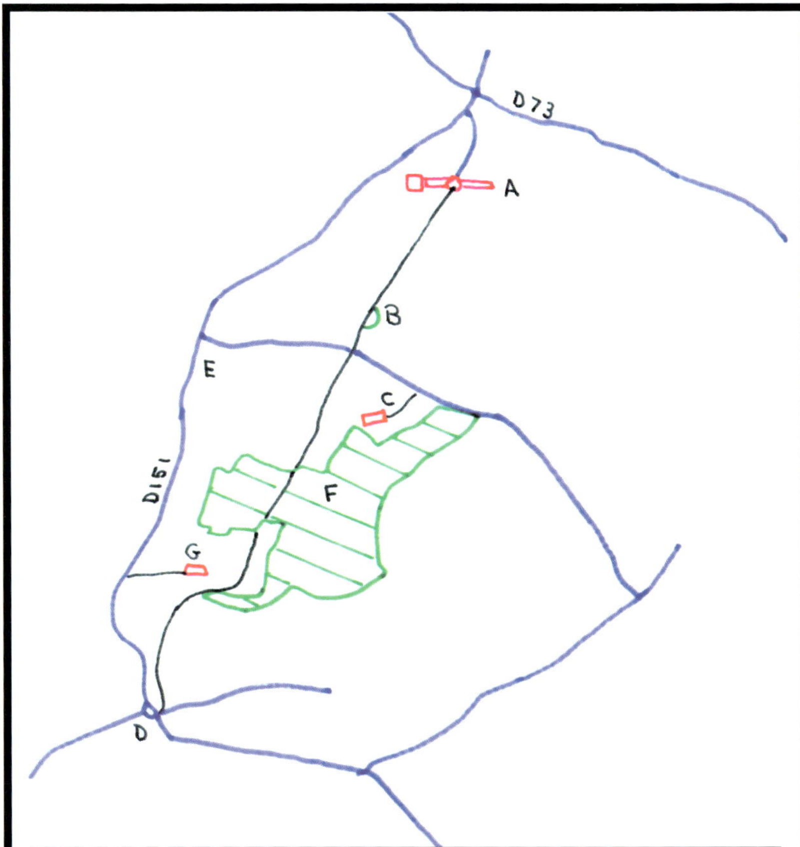

Route 1st July Walk

A THIEPVAL MEMORIAL
B GRANATLOCH
C LONSDALE CEMETERY
D CRUCIFIX CORNER
E AUTHUILLE
F AUTHILLE WOOD
G BLIGHTY VALLEY CEMETERY

Map not to scale showing 1st July attack

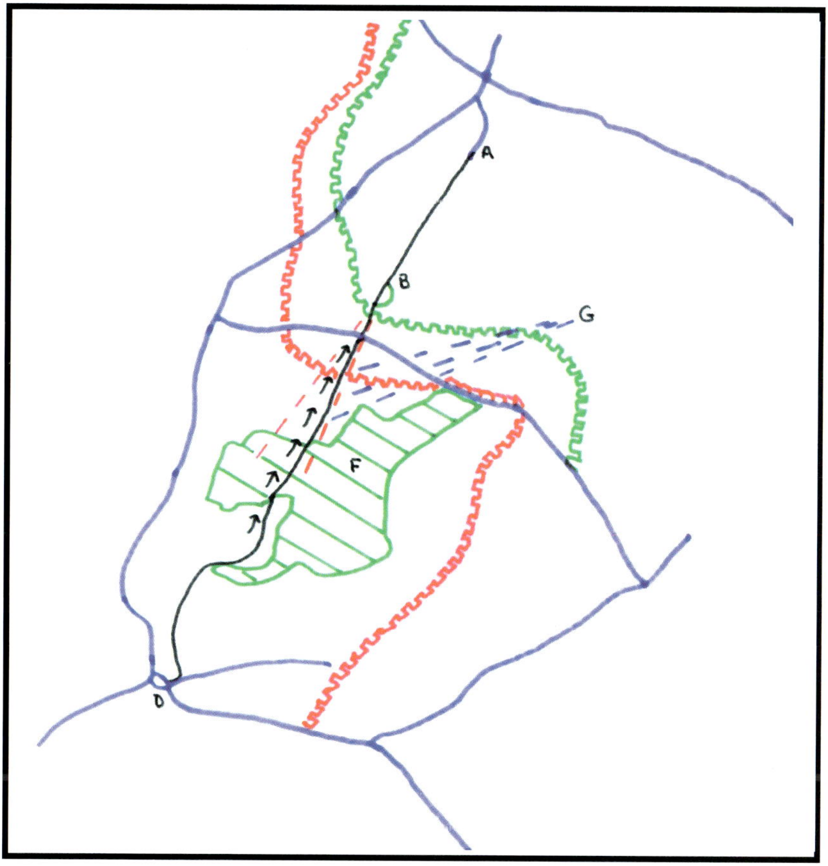

The red zigzag line represents British Frontline 1st July 1916

The green zigzag line represents German Frontline 1st July 1916

Black arrows show Lonsdales route towards *Granatloch* B

Red dotted line shows direction of German fire from *Granatloch* B

Blue dotted line shows direction of German fire from *Nordwerk* G

A - Thiepval F - Authuille Wood D - Crucifix Corner

Step by step guide

The black lines represent the track and the outline of Authuille wood. The blue lines represent road systems D151 Crucifix Corner to Authuille.

1. Start at A **(Thiepval Memorial)**

2. Go to B **(Granatloch)**

3. Go to C **(Lonsdale Cemetery)**

4. Go to back towards B then turn left head towards D

5. Go to D **(Crucifix Corner)**

Once you reach Crucifix Corner you have completed the tour. You can then either retrace the route back to Thiepval, or follow the D151 towards Authuille, (please beware of fast local traffic). When you finally reach Authuille continue on the main road, just as you leave the village you will see on your right a road signed Lonsdale Cemetery. Follow the sign; the road rises steeply until you eventually reach the track from where you came earlier. Turn left and return to Thiepval Memorial.

18th November tour

Unfortunately for those wishing to visit the November battlefield, the sheer geographical nature of Redan Ridge and the lack of good roads and tracks rather restricts a tour on the lines of the 1st July route. Never the less it is still possible to visit the area and cemeteries spread along the ridge.

START

An ideal place to start would be to drive to the village of Serre; then park and walk. The only cemetery in Serre that contains graves of Hereford Lonsdales is Serre Road No1; here you will find the graves of three former Herefords.

Serre Road No 1 Cemetery (Author's collection 2005)

(Author's collection 2005)

Just across the road from Serre Road No1 Cemetery, you should see the CWGC sign indicating the route to 5 of the Redan Ridge cemeteries. You can walk but you may wish to consider driving, stopping off to walk to the desired cemetery you choose to visit. If you remain on this road you will eventually make your way into the village of Beaumont-Hamel, where you will see CWGC signs indicating Frankfort Trench Cemetery. To visit Ten Tree Alley Cemetery I would advise you to return to Serre and carry on along the main road. Just after you leave Serre you will see a CWGC sign on your right indicating the route to Ten Tree Alley. Follow this sign, you will after a short drive see the cemetery on your left, however you will have to park and walk along the grass pathway to reach the cemetery.

Grass track leading to Ten Tree Alley Cemetery (Author's collection 2005)

Ten Tree Alley is believed to be the farthest that men from the 97th Brigade advanced on 18th November 1916. Four of the men of the Border Regiment are Hereford Lonsdales.

After you leave the cemeteries continue along the road and you will eventually arrive at Beaumont-Hamel. Turn left and just a few yards on your left you should see the CWGC sign for New Munich Trench. This is the last of the Redan Ridge cemeteries on our tour dedicated to the 18th November attack.

New Munich Trench Cemetery (Author's collection 2005)

From New Munich Trench the visitor can get a good view across Redan Ridge, and you can pick out a number of the other cemeteries in the distance. After you leave the cemetery return to the main road and turn right.

There are a number of interesting sites close by to visit, such as Hawthorn Crater the site of a large mine detonated just minutes before the 1st July attack. Look out for the large white stone Celtic cross on your right. Park here and you will find Hawthorn Crater just over the road. If you then head for the village of Auchonvillers will see the signs for Avril Williams' tea rooms, here you can get a light meal or snack as well as hot and cold drinks.

The New Walk

Since 2005, I have spent many hours walking and researching the area connected with the attack of 18th November 1916. This additional walk covers many of the key areas and will hopefully give the reader a feel for the terrain over which the battle took place. (You need to allow yourself 3- 3 ½ hours)

Start at Avril Williams' tea rooms in Auchonvillers its best to check first that leaving your vehicle is okay, however if this is a problem drive up the road approximately 300 yards' in the direction of Newfoundland park and you should see a pull-in on the left close to some farm buildings. Just passed this pull-in you will see a track on your left follow this track downhill until you reach the D163 Auchonvillers to Beaumont-Hamel road at this point turn right and walk down the road towards Beaumont-Hamel.

As you walk down hill you should see on your left a track which leads up to the Argyll & Sutherland Highlanders Memorial, take this track and head up to the memorial

Track to memorial (Author's collection 2011)

Once you have looked at the memorial continue walking up the Sunken Road. On the 1st July 1916 the Sunken Road was approximately midway between the British and German frontlines in No Man's Land. It was used by British troops and if you look carefully in the bank sides on your right as you walk up you can still make out the entrances to dugouts.

Sunken Road (Author's collection 2011)

Once you have reached the top of the lane turn right and walk along the track. As you walk along this track may wish to visit the 3 small battlefield cemeteries Redan Ridge numbers 1-3-2, continue down the track until you eventually come to a metalled section of road. Turn right and walk down hill after approximately 250 yards turn left onto the Rue de Serre, after approximately another 400 yards you should join Wagon Road. Turn left, you are now standing in Wagon road where the attack of November 18th started off from, continue up the road following the CWGC signs for Wagon Road Cemetery.

Wagon Road Cemetery (Author's collection 2011)

After you leave Wagon Road Cemetery, continue up the road until you reach Munich Trench Cemetery.

Munich Trench Cemetery (Author's collection 2011)

More detail regarding the cemeteries and the men buried within can be found in the CWGC registers placed in the bronze cabinets built into the gate posts.

Retrace your steps back down Wagon Road and continue until you eventually reach the village of Beaumont-Hamel, now turn right and head up the road (D163) after just a few yards on your right you will see a flagpole which commemorates the capture of the village on 13th November 1916 by the 51st Highland Division. Continue up the road back towards Auchonvillers after approximately 700 yards look for the signs on your left for Hawthorn Crater.

Steps to Hawthorn Crater (Author's collection 2011)

Take care as you ascend the steps and walk up the path to the wooded area on the crest of the ridge, keep to the right and as you walk around the outside you can glimpse in at several points and view what remains of Hawthorn Crater.

There are in fact two craters the first was detonated at 07.20hrs on the 1st July 1916 ten minutes before the main attack took place. 40,600lbs (in excess of 18tons) of ammonal high explosive was used and a crater measuring 40ft deep and over 300ft wide was created.
Thc German position on the ridge know as Hawthorn Ridge Redoubt was totally destroyed by the blast, however thc Germans managed to hold on to their side of the crater and by the end of the day the British were forced to abandon the area. At 0545hrs on the 13th November 1916 another charge of 30,000lbs (in excess of 13tons) was blown forming the second crater. This attack proved more successful and led to the 51st Division steadily advancing and eventually capturing the village of Beaumont-Hamel.

Hawthorn Crater on ridge (Author's collection 2011)

Now bear right and after approximately 20 yards join the track that leads to Hawthorn Ridge No 1 Cemetery.

Hawthorn Ridge Cemetery No1 (Author's collection 2011)

After visiting the cemetery rejoin the track and continue walking straight on, Newfoundland Park should be on your left hand side, after approximately 250 yards take the track to your right and follow it down until you eventually rejoin the track where you started the walk. Turn left and walk back up this track and into Auchonvillers.
Once back in Auchonvillers I suggest you take some time to visit the museum at Avril Williams' Tea Rooms.
This is in my opinion a first class museum and has many artefacts' from both WW1 and WW2, once a private collection Avril has continued to develop and extend the collection.
To the rear of the tea rooms can be found an original trench line which has been excavated and leads into a cellar system beneath the property that was used as a dressing station.
This is also a good opportunity to have some refreshments before continuing on with further visits.

Roll of Honour of men from the 3/1st Herefordshire Regiment Who Served with the 11th Bn Border Regiment The Lonsdales

ROLL OF HONOUR
OF MEN FROM THE HEREFORDSHIRE REGIMENT WHO DIED WHILST SERVING WITH THE 11TH BN BORDER REGIMENT

NAME	RANK	NO	DIED	BURIED
AYRES WILLIAM JEFFRIES	A/SGT	27668	10-07-17	NIEUPORT
BEDELL CHARLES EDWARD	PTE	27710	18-11-16	THIEPVAL
BEVAN JAMES	PTE	27768	12-01-17	EUSTON-RD
BEVAN JOHN	PTE	27706	24-11-16	PORT-DE-PARIS
BOUNDS BENJAMIN	PTE	27853	18-11-16	WAGON-RD
BOWEN WILFRED LODOWICK	PTE	27715	18-11-16	FRANKFORT-T
BRIDGE ROBERT JOHN	L/CPL	27670	02-12-17	TYNE-COT
BRISBOURNE GRAHAM OSCAR	PTE	27707	18-11-16	THIEPVAL
BROOKE FREDRICK JAMES	L/CPL	27842	18-11-16	WAGON-RD
BROOKES THOMAS	PTE	27716	18-11-16	WAGON-RD
CHANT HERBERT	PTE	27718	12-01-17	EUSTON-RD
CLARKE WILLIAM CHARLES	PTE	27717	08-04-18	HAMBURG CEM
CLOSE JAMES	PTE	27722	18-11-16	WAGON-RD
COLBURN HENRY	PTE	27724	18-11-16	SERRE RD NO 1
COLEMAN HERBERT	PTE	27721	18-11-16	THIEPVAL
COWDELL ARTHUR SAMUEL	PTE	27720	18-11-16	WAGON-RD
DAVIES DAVID	PTE	27729	21-05-17	VALENCIENNES
DAVIES GEORGE	PTE	27732	18-11-16	WAGON-RD
DAVIES GEORGE HENRY	PTE	27727	03-01-17	HARGICOURT
DAVIES JAMES	PTE	27730	18-11-16	SERRE RD NO 1
DAVIES PHILIP LLEWELLYN	PTE	27857	18-11-16	THIEPVAL
DAVIES THOMAS GILBERT	PTE	27726	28-03-17	HOME
DAVIS REGINALD RICHARD	PTE	27731	18-11-16	WAGON-RD
DAW HARRY JAMES	PTE	27734	18-11-16	TEN TREE ALLE
DUTTON HORACE FREDRICK	PTE	27675	31-01-17	UNICORN CEM
EAST LEWIS JOHN	PTE	27737	18-11-16	WAGON-RD
FARMER FREDRICK	PTE	27744	18-11-16	THIEPVAL
GOUGH ERNEST HAROLD	PTE	27750	28-03-17	HAMBURG CEM
GRIFFITHS THOMAS	PTE	27849	18-11-16	WAGON-RD
GRIFFITHS WILLIAM	PTE	27752	17-12-16	PORT-DE-CALIS
GRIFFITHS WILLIAM HENERY	PTE	27751	18-11-16	WAGON-RD
GRUBHAM GEORGE	PTE	27745	18-11-16	THIEPVAL
HAINES GEORGE ALBERT	PTE	27756	18-11-16	WARLOY BAILL
HALL EDWARD WILLIAM	PTE	27760	18-11-16	WAGON-RD
HAMBLIN REGINALD W	PTE	27757	18-11-16	WAGON-RD
HAMMOND VINCIENT E	PTE	27767	18-11-16	FRANKFORT-T
HARRIS WILLIAM	PTE	27755	18-11-16	WAGON-RD
HERBERT EDWARD CHARLES	PTE	27859	18-11-16	THIEPVAL
HICKS ALBERT EDWARD	PTE	27758	18-11-16	WAGON-RD

ROLL OF HONOUR
OF MEN FROM THE HEREFORDSHIRE REGIMENT WHO DIED WHILST SERVING WITH THE 11TH BN BORDER REGIMENT

NAME	RANK	NO	DIED	BURIED
HOLBROOK CHARLES	PTE	27766	18-11-16	THIEPVAL
HOLDER ALFRED HENRY	PTE	27680	18-11-16	THIEPVAL
HOPE WALTER ERNEST	PTE	27860	01-04-17	SAVAY BRIT
HUGHES ALBERT JOSHEPH	PTE	27681	18-11-16	THIEPVAL
HUGHES FREDRICK	PTE	27761	18-11-16	SERRE-RD NO 1
JACKSON GEORGE HENERY	A/CPL	27682	18-11-16	THIEPVAL
JAMES WILLIAM	PTE	27787	18-11-16	THIEPVAL
KENDRICK WILLIAM	PTE	27772	10-02-17	ANCRE CEM
KINNERSLEY THOMAS	PTE	27771	14-04-17	THIEPVAL
KITSON ALBERT	PTE	27773	14-04-17	FORESTE CEM
LANCELEY JAMES	PTE	27865	10-07-17	NIEUPORT MEM
LEWIS ALBERT BENJAMIN	PTE	27867	03-08-17	ETAPES CEM
LEWIS THOMAS	PTE	27777	06-04-17	THIEPVAL
MADDOX THOMAS EDMUND	PTE	27683	12-01-17	EUSTON RD
MALSOM WILLIAM	L/CPL	27784	18-11-16	TEN TREE ALLE
MARTIN JOHN	PTE	27778	18-11-16	THIEPVAL
MEEK LONAL JAMES	PTE	27785	18-11-16	WAGON-RD
MOUND EDWARD	PTE	27868	18-11-16	MUNICH TRENC
NASH ROWLAND	PTE	27739	18-11-16	THIEPVAL
NEVETT JOHN DENNIS	PTE	27791	18-11-16	WAGON RD
NICHOLAS EDWARD	PTE	27793	15-12-16	BERLIN CEM
NICHOLAS FREDRICK G	PTE	27790	18-11-16	TEN TREE ALLE
NICHOLS CHARLES THOMAS	PTE	27704	18-11-16	THIEPVAL
OWENS DAVID EVAN	PTE	27684	18-11-16	TEN TREE ALLE
PARTON ARTHUR DAVID	PTE	27872	10-01-17	THIEPVAL
PERKINS ALBERT GEORGE	PTE	27807	28-05-17	HAMBURG CEM
PHILLIPS WILLIAM HENRY	PTE	27802	18-11-16	WAGON-RD
PHILPS FREDRICK GEORGE	PTE	27810	18-11-16	THIEPVAL
PINCHES STANLEY WILLIAM	PTE	27870	10-07-17	NIEUPORT CEM
PITT WILLIAM THOMAS	PTE	27688	18-11-16	REDAN RIDGE 3
POWELL FREDERICK	PTE	27837	01-04-17	SAVY BRIT CEM
POWELL JOHN THOMAS	L/CPL	27808	02-12-17	TYNE COT MEM
RUSSELL JOHN	PTE	27815	01-04-17	SAVY BRIT CEM
SEAGER JOHN PERCY	PTE	27822	14-04-17	THIEPVAL
SMITH HEGER GEORGE M	PTE	27877	18-11-16	THIEPVAL
STEPHENS BERTIE	PTE	27691	12-01-17	WAGON-RD
STOKES ALBERT EDWARD	PTE	27692	18-11-16	THIEPVAL
TARBATH FRANCIS GEORGE	PTE	27829	18-11-16	THIEPVAL
THOMPSON ALBERT LOUIS	PTE	27828	18-11-16	ST SEVER ROUE

TRUMPER WILLIAM	PTE	27823	27-11-16	MONT-HUON
TUNLEY JAMES	PTE	27680	01-04-17	SAVY BRIT CEM
TURNER HENERY	PTE	27814	22-12-18	LES BARAQUES
VAUGHAN JOHN	PTE	27879	11-12-17	THIEPVAL
WALKER ALBAN	PTE	27698	12-01-17	EUSTON RD
WALKER ROBERT HARRY	PTE	27830	18-11-16	THIEPVAL
WALL GEORGE	PTE	27328	28-02-17	THIEPVAL
WALL THOMAS	PTE	27697	18-11-16	WAGON-RD
WILCOX JOSEPH THOMAS	PTE	27834	10-07-17	NIEUPORT CEM
WILKINS HARRY	PTE	27938	27-11-16	ETAPES
WITCOMB ERNEST GEORGE	PTE	27696	18-11-16	THIEPVAL
WOOTON WILLIAM	PTE	27837	18-11-16	THIEPVAL
WRIGHT HAROLD GEORGE	PTE	27840	18-11-16	MUNICH TRENC
YEMM THOMAS HENRY	PTE	27841	18-11-16	THIEPVAL

This Roll of Honour has been compiled from official lists and Soldiers Died in the Great War database[20], inevitably an individual may be missed from such lists or information such as spelling of names etc may sometimes be incorrect. I apologise for any such omissions or mistakes and once notified will endeavour to correct.

The total number of men killed or died whilst serving with the 11th Border Regiment throughout the Great war was 792 of this number 92 were former members of the Herefordshire Regiment + 2 ex Kings Shropshire Light Infantry.

In total 148 11th Borderers 'Lonsdales' were killed in action on 18-11-16 more would die of wounds in the following days and months, this figure includes 60 ex Herefordshire men.

In total 162 16th Highland Light Infantry were killed in action 18-11-16 more would die from wounds in the following days and months.

---

[20] Soldiers Died in the Great War searchable digital database, constructed by The Naval & Military Press.

It would not have been possible for me to have completed this work without the tireless patience and understanding of my wife Sharon. I would also like to take this opportunity to express my sincere thanks to my daughter Georgina Morgan for her artwork and to my good friends in particular, Nic Christian who accompanied me on several field trips to France and contributed many of the photographs. I would also like to thank Dave Ormesher, Peter John and Nic Dinsdale Head of Humanities Lady Hawkins School Kington who kindly helped with proof reading and technical guidance. Lastly it has to be said that the contributions made by relatives of many of the men featured in this work has been invaluable.

Bibliography

Somme. Lyn Macdonald. (Penguin Books 1983)

The Somme Battlefields. Martin & Mary Middlebrook. (Penguin Books 1994)

Thiepval Somme. Michael Stedman. (Leo Cooper 1995)

Battlefields of the First World War. Major & Mrs Holt. (Pavilion Books Ltd 1993)

The First Day On The Somme. Martin Middlebrook. (Penguin Books 2001)

The Battle Of The Somme A Topographical History. G Gliddon. (Sutton Publishing 1996)

Epic Actions of the First World War. R W Gould MBE. (Tom Donovan Pub 1997)

The Somme The Day-By-Day-Account. Chris McCarthy. (Arms & Armour Press 1993)

A Saga of Scotland history of the 16th HLI. Thomas Chalmers. (J McCallum & Co)

War Diaries of the 11th Bn Border Regiment, July – November 1916, and the 16th and 17th Bns Highland Light Infantry November 1916.

Abbreviations

Adj (Adjutant)

Bn (Battalion) Bde (Brigade)

Brig/ Gen(Brigadier or Brigadier General)

CO (Commanding Officer)

Col/Lt/Col (Colonel or Lieutenant Colonel)

Cpl/ L-Cpl (Corporal/ Lance Corporal)

Capt (Captain)

CSM (Company Sergeant Major)

CWGC (Commonwealth War Graves Commission)

DCM (Distinguished Conduct Medal) DSO (Distinguished Service Order)

Lt/S/Lt (Lieutenant or Second Lieutenant)

Maj (Major)

MC (Military Cross) MIC (Mention in despatches) MM (Military Medal)

MO (Medical Officer)

SDGW (Soldiers Died In the Great War)

Sgt (Sergeant)

Sqd (Squadron)

Grace C. Lonsdale
1928
Lonsdale

Notes

Notes

Notes

Notes